To my friends and spiritual/natural family—It is because of the lessons and edification that I gained from you that I am here today. You will never be forgotten.

To Niche
From Amber
Gardner

This book is a memoir. It reflects my present recollections of experiences over time. Some names and characteristics have been changed, some events have been compressed, and some dialogue has been recreated.

BIGGER
Than Me

A story of struggle, surrender, and grace

AMBER GARDNER

Bigger Than Me
Copyright © 2018 by Amber Gardner. All rights reserved.

Editing, book design, and cover design by Next Page, LLC

Published in the United States on October 1, 2018
ISBN- 10: 0-578-43966-2
ISBN- 13: 978-0-578-43966-2

All rights reserved. No part of the material protected by this copyright may be reproduced or utilized in any form by any means, electronic or mechanical, including photocopying, recording, or by any information storage and retrieval system without permission in writing from the copyright owner. Contact Amber Gardner for permission to make copies of any part of this work.

CONTENTS

Prologue 1

1. Set Apart 3
2. "Home Sweet Home?" 7
3. Eye-Opening Experiences 11
4. Introduction to My Achilles' Heel 17
5. Confessions of a Pew Baby (Pt. 1) 21
6. Confessions of Pew Baby (Pt. 2) 25
7. Self-Inflicted Wounds 29
8. R-E-S-P-*I*-C-T 35
9. Bad Branding 39
10. Wake-Up Call (Pt. 1) 45
11. Wake-Up Call (Pt. 2) 51
12. Reunion 55
13. Called to Change 63

14. Victories in the Valley 69

15. "Mustard Seed" Miracle 75

16. Kingdom Connections 81

17. Won't He Do It? 85

18. When It Rains, It Pours 89

19. With Favor Comes Responsibility 93

20. Kingdom Kindness 97

21. Stepping Into Submission 103

22. Epilogue (Bigger Than Me) 109

23. Acknowledgements 111

PROLOGUE

According to the Merriam-Webster Dictionary, *destiny* is "a predetermined course of events often held to be an irresistible power or agency." Looking at this definition now, after overcoming various challenges in my life, I can truly say that it holds fast to its true meaning. Every trial I have survived, every test that has become a testimony, and every struggle that has strengthened me was intended to lead me to my predetermined purpose. However, it took a long time for me to fully understand that. For many years, I mixed up my destiny with my dreams.

Now, the Merriam-Webster Dictionary also defines *dream* as "a strongly desired goal or purpose." For a long time, my dreams and desires controlled me. From my desire to live a "stable" life, to my dream to be loved, to even my craving for approval, these things consumed my focus and ran my life for years, and many times they did not drive me in the direction of my true destiny.

I was so determined to do things my own way and trust my own instincts that I refused to realize that I was not following my true calling. By the grace and mercy of God, I was given time to recognize that His way, not my way, was the answer. Thankfully, all of my experiences, even the additional ones my decisions created, were able to be used for my purpose, which is why I am sharing them—in order to help others reach their destinies.

At the end of the day, it's not about me or my accomplishments. The focus of this book is not how many times I have won or the amount of success I have seen. The sole objective is to help others fulfill the destinies that God has ordained for them. Once one begins fulfilling their destiny, other things can move forward. Everything that they are destined to do, every mission they are supposed to help complete, and every person they are intended to aid will be able to benefit from crossing their path—once that path is correct.

So, in the following pages, I will be sharing how I learned through my experiences what my path was and how I came to the realization that my calling and my life is *bigger than me.*

SET APART

It felt like a dream. My conscious had still not truly digested the fact that I, Amber Brianna Kathlene Gardner, had been granted this amazing opportunity. If anyone had told me that in a year I would go from being homeless with a 2.89 GPA to being accepted to over ten colleges and universities and offered over $100,000 in scholarships, then I would have said they were crazy.

That's the great thing about God moving you towards your destiny. Sometimes it will completely knock you off your feet. Just thinking about it still puts a smile on my face, because I know it was nothing but His grace and favor that allowed all of it to come to pass.

As I looked around and saw the other young ladies I was sitting next to, I knew I was set apart. I still had not fully accepted it, but, thankfully, God already had a plan set up to correct that. The first step was to get me to the place where much of my growth was ordained to occur, which is why He allowed me to be accepted to and receive a Presidential Scholarship from one of the greatest Historically Black Colleges and Universities (HBCUs) in the country, Hampton University.

Now, this miracle was not sitting alone at the table of my life during that year. I was also able to meet and sing for President Barack and First Lady Michelle Obama, enjoy an amazing graduation party, stay in my own place, rent-free, for roughly two months, receive a shopping spree at Target for everything I needed for my dorm room and closet, and receive a free laptop computer. It did not just rain blessings in my life during that season. It poured!

This is why I have grown thankful for the struggles I've been through, because they opened the door for God to show His greatness. Not only was I able to benefit from them, but it gave me the opportunity to share the God I serve with others. You know what they say, "You need a test to have a testimony."

Now, it took time and maturity for me to wrap my mind around the fact that God wanted my testimony to be shared with my classmates, teachers, and others who crossed my path. Even though He had moved miraculously in my life, my desire to fit in and the shame I felt from my mother and me still being homeless at the time led me to hold my tongue with most of the people in my life for some months. I felt it was best to blend in, but God had other plans.

So, as I sat in Ogden Hall with my new Hampton sisters, taking in my life's new path, God was already preparing and planting the gold nuggets I would discover while traveling down it. That's one thing that I could not deny even when I doubted God. No matter what, He always had blessings and pieces of wisdom for me along my journey. Whether I was climbing to the top of a mountain or stumbling to the bottom of the valley, there were some jewels for me to gather along the way.

Thankfully, I have been collecting jewels of wisdom since I was a young girl. I have not always recognized it, but rather than holding that against me, God uses it for His glory. If I had recognized every single blessing, I may not have encountered certain challenges which helped me grow and share my testimony with others.

Now, this testimony starts way before my time at Hampton University. It begins in the early 2000's, roughly twelve years earlier, with one simple move. As a result of my family moving from Virginia to Connecticut, many things shifted, and my life would never be the same.

"HOME SWEET HOME?"

The idea of *home* is an interesting thing. If one was to go from person to person regarding this term, everything, from the definition, to the location, to even the level of importance, would change. One person may say that home is where you grow up, while another may disagree, claiming that it is where one feels safe enough to be himself. For one individual, the location may be Chicago or New York City, while home for someone else may be a small city or town most of us have never even heard of. Finally, one person may say it is one of the most important things in her life because it helped her through many challenges, but another person may consider it worth nothing since he never had one.

As a child, I considered home one of the most important things in my life. Up until I was around six years old, going home was like taking a vacation. I felt happiness, what I *thought* was joy and peace, and comfort whenever I was there. Now, because my mother worked days and my father worked nights, I spent more time with him and became a true daddy's girl. I idolized my father. I did not see that idolization as an issue then, but looking back, I now see where the danger lay.

The Merriam-Webster Dictionary states to *idolize* is to worship as a god or to love or admire to excess. Either way one looks at it, this could be unhealthy and keep a person from their calling or purpose because they are so focused on that person that they forget to be themselves. God cannot use you when you are unknowingly following someone else. This is why I see that one of the reasons God had my family move was to place us in a setting that would show me that my father was still under construction.

You see, I subconsciously viewed my father as perfect. Because I had so much in common with him, from my love for singing and music, to my sense of humor, to even my outspoken personality, I felt no one could understand me better than him. However, what I did not realize is that the Creator of the formula understands the results far better than one of the factors used. Once that is understood, the Creator receives the credit and can aid in keeping the results pure or restoring them to their intended state if they are tampered with.

When my parents and I moved from Virginia to their home state, Connecticut, I did not really know how my life was about to shift. My fairytale perception of one's walk with Christ was getting ready to be completely cracked open and flipped on its head. I could no longer view God as a parent who spoiled me by saying, "Yes!" whenever I made a request. He had to show me that not only was my father not perfect, but neither was one's journey of salvation.

For me to be used by Him and fulfill the destiny that was assigned to me, the learning process had to begin. As many people say, "Experience is the best teacher."

So, we moved in with my Aunt Rachel in New Britain, Connecticut in 2001, and I'll admit that as a recently baptized six-year-old girl, I was curious about what God had for me in this next chapter of my life. Even though I knew I would miss my friends and church, I wondered what I would discover and be exposed to in Connecticut. Ironically, rather than just being introduced to northern winters and city life, I was shown much more.

You see, everyone does not tell you that gold has to be put in the fire to be purified or that a diamond has to be worked on and cut to shine bright and be considered a jewel. I only heard about the end results, but I did not know that grief may come before glory. Well, mine began slowly, but surely, and it started right at home.

EYE-OPENING EXPERIENCES

Two parts of my personality that have been around forever are my desire to voice my opinion and my ability to comprehend things. I remember having a conversation with my father after church when I was little. My pastor at the time had preached a sermon about something and I was telling my father what I had understood from the message. By the end of our conversation, my dad was calling for my mom to come into the room with us because he could not believe I had digested and understood so much.

Due to my passion for sharing my views and my gift of comprehension, moments like that occurred pretty regularly. However, what do you do when your eyes are opened to things you would rather stay blind to? How do you figure out if you should tell someone what you know or remain silent? Well, I figured out that those two questions can only be answered by God.

Also, the fairytale perspective I had regarding my walk with Christ began to dramatically shift because I learned that God is not a "yes man." Sometimes, the answer to your prayer will simply be, "No." As Isaiah 55:8 says, "'My thoughts are nothing like your thoughts,' says the LORD. 'And my ways are beyond anything you could imagine.'" Simply put, God knows best.

As my parents became readjusted to their home state, I tried my best to embrace my new surroundings. Slowly, I began to notice tensions rising within our family. Arguments began growing more hostile and voices were raised more often. It was like dysfunction was an overnight guest who wanted to become a new, permanent roommate.

Being a child, outspoken or not, I wanted to stay in my place regarding my parent's marriage. So, I simply observed and hoped the dysfunction would cease. However, instead of the unwanted guest leaving and turning in his key, he signed a lease and moved in with some more roommates: physical fighting and addiction.

You see, like a lot of children, I had no idea of my father's trials or the thorns in his flesh. However, surroundings and timing can make almost anything come back to the surface; I don't care how long it has been buried or how deep you buried it. So, looking back on things as an adult, I can easily see how our family, the surroundings, and our adjusting to the fresh move resulted in alcoholism making a surprise return with its gifts of dysfunction, confusion, and strife, along with numerous suitcases of baggage that I doubt anyone expected.

This is why I was shocked when I had to make the decision between what was comfortable and what was right at such a young age. However, I did what I felt I had to do in order to honor my family. So, I decided to tell my Aunt Rachel, the owner of the house, that my father and mother were now having physical altercations along with verbal disagreements.

I guess at that age I still viewed things as being very simple or black and white. My thought process basically was, "The quicker it gets out, the quicker it gets fixed." What I did not know was that the only way that strategy can work is if everyone keeps everything out in the open. The minute someone starts covering stuff back up or keeping problems to themselves, more issues start. Secrecy only feeds the drama and dysfunction even more.

So, since everyone was not thrilled to snatch the covers off of the situation, it was subconsciously or unintentionally nursed to grow stronger. Every argument, every misunderstanding, and every night an argument was not solved added fuel to the fire, and everyone knows if you keep adding fuel to a fire it can burn out of control, which is what began to happen to our family. Thankfully, God is the living water that can put the fire out—once you let Him.

As the years went on and things continued to repeat and worsen, my relationship with God took a severe hit. I began to feel like every day that I attended a church service, every week that I went with my parents to a choir rehearsal, every time I testified, every day and night I read my Bible, every time I prayed, every time I talked about God to a family member or classmate, and every day that I served God was in vain. My frustration, anger, and hurt were very hard to bear, not only because of the situation, but also because of what the anger was truly covering up.

Subconsciously, I felt like there was no point in drawing closer to God because there was no point in sharing Him with others. I felt like there was no point in telling others about what God could do for them if He wasn't doing what *I* needed Him to. However, I learned much later that we have to trust that God knows what is best. As Hebrews 11:1 states, "Now faith is the substance of things hoped for, the evidence of things not seen" (KJV).

On the other side of things, my parents' relationship was experiencing the same increased distance and dysfunction as my relationship with Christ. The fights continued, the arguments rarely ceased, and the tension grew until finally, in 2004, my parents decided to get a divorce. My mother and I moved into a shelter for mothers and children who were transitioning or going through times of change with their families.

From the little that I can remember about that place, the experience was not terrible at all. The people were incredibly friendly, the room that we shared with another mother and daughter was nice, and some of the workers even made sandwiches for my mother and me once when we were going with our church on a road trip to New York. It was a pleasant, warm experience and a time of rest.

After approximately six months there, my mom and I then found a wonderful townhome. It was a great place. Not only was it quaint, comfy, and inviting, but more importantly, it was ours. There was even a building in the area for children to come to after school. Inside, there was a TV and games like pool. There was even a basketball court.

Also, we had great neighbors who showed amazing love. I, being the sociable person that I am, made friends quickly with a brother and sister who had a lovely mother. She was in a wheelchair, but it did not matter to me because she had a heart of gold. Plus, their mother having a physical issue helped them relate to me even more. I mean, most children do not understand what it is like to have a mother who can have a life-threatening seizure at any moment.

Many people would not know this when looking at my mother, but she has been struggling with a seizure disorder since she was a teenager. Now, for those of you who do not know, a *seizure* is defined as, "the physical manifestations (as convulsions, sensory disturbances, or loss of consciousness) resulting from abnormal electrical discharges in the brain...." Initially, she only had these episodes when she was asleep; however, she eventually began having seizures while she was awake, too.

Because God has given me a personality that exceeds my age, the seizures themselves did not initially bother me. My parents were married, so even though it scared and worried me when they would happen, there was always someone else there to help manage things. However, all of that changed when my parents divorced. Once that happened, the load went from being on my father's shoulders to being on mine.

Now, don't get me wrong. She was the mother of his child, a woman of God, and he had known her for over ten years, so my father did care about my mother's health. But since he no longer lived with us following their divorce, the responsibility of caring for her when these seizures took place fell on the person who lived with her: me.

INTRODUCTION TO MY ACHILLES' HEEL

In the Merriam-Webster Dictionary, a *caretaker* is defined as, "one that gives physical or emotional care and support," and the phrase used for the example describes one who, "served as caretaker to the younger children." It is actually a bit more than coincidental for to me to see that example, because caring for my mother felt like a never-ending battle for many years.

You see, I initially viewed my mother's condition as an important responsibility. It showed its face occasionally, but it was something that I felt I could handle. However, being young and still partially naive, I did not know that everyone, even Jesus himself, has to endure seasons of isolation and that season does not guarantee that your problems will go away. Some thorns will remain even when it is only you and God.

For me, that is what those late nights at the hospital with my mom felt like. Due to the pressure, I subconsciously found the silver lining or silver "specks" in the cloud. I would tell myself that I could watch cable and access Wi-Fi while I was in there, and amusingly enough, even now I use these facts as "pick-me-ups" when my mother has to go to the hospital due to a seizure.

Unfortunately, when you still don't know what love is and how God designed it to be, you can develop a tainted replica of it. This is why, in my mind, caring for my mother when she had a seizure went from being a responsibility to feeling like a burden.

Since I was an only child who was used to receiving all of the attention and constantly compared herself to other children, I felt that having to handle all of this was unfair. To me, since other young people didn't have this weight on their shoulders, I shouldn't have to carry it, either. What I didn't realize was that God gives us weight not according to our comfort level, but according to our strength.

Sadly, since I wasn't viewing things from that perspective, I became blind to the fact that my feelings toward God had shifted terribly. As the years went by, my view of our Savior continued to subside. Rather than thinking, "I know He will!" my thoughts went to, "I think He might?" and ended at, "I know He won't."

See, everyone has an Achilles heel or place where they are weak. For one person, it may be that they struggle to understand things. Mine, however, is the complete opposite. Rather than having the problem of not understanding enough, there has been a tug of war caused by understanding too much. Due to my intelligence and desire to understand more, I rarely wondered, "Can God do it?" because I knew He was able. So, my beef with God was not rooted in the fact that He couldn't change things, but that God *chose* not to change things.

It's as if a child asks for an iPhone for Christmas and their parent or guardian cannot afford it, so they get them a pre-paid cellphone. The child may have an easier time understanding that because the adult is unable to do it. Now, if the parent or guardian is a millionaire and does the exact same thing, the child may have a fit because the adult has the money and still won't fulfill their wish. In my mind, God was the millionaire parent or guardian who chose to say "No," even when He had the means.

Of course, like any self-dug pit, this hole took time to grow. Initially, I had no issues with or against God. I read my Bible regularly and prayed almost every night. Then, my parents began having marital problems. So, naturally, I started to pray that God would save their marriage. Now, I did not know at that time that every prayer that is brought before God will not get a "Yes." Just because God can do it does not mean it is in His divine will for it to be done. In other words, what looks good is not always good for you.

God knew that my parents being together was not best for any of us, so He did not improve their marriage. Since I did not recognize this, I continued to ask God to fix their relationship. As I kept praying and their marriage continued rotting, I began to develop a grudge against God.

Yes, the pew-baby who loved Christ and church developed a grudge against God. To me, my dedication, relationship, and knowledge of God should've been enough for my prayers to be answered the way I wanted. However, looking back on it, I see that God did what was best. See, God has to expose where your loyalty truly lies. Who needs "fair weather" people serving them? You have to be willing to take up your cross and follow Him, no matter what has to be crucified in the process.

Once my mother and I returned to Virginia, the poisonous seeds that were already planted began to be watered by tears of frustration, anger, and distress, along with other things. My anger with God began to expand as my path continued to become an obstacle course that I felt forced to complete.

For one, the swing of abandonment from my father was added to the course. One moment, I would receive a call and be happy at high heights. Then, we would get into an argument or "misunderstanding," as people sometimes like to put it, and be low, almost touching the ground, hoping that my strength or God's divine wind could push me back forward.

Then, I was having to face climbing the wall of acceptance. You see, I was struggling heavily with trying to fit in. Now, I know that a lot of believers are probably thinking, "God's children are supposed to be set apart. So that's a good thing." However, my situation was a bit more complicated. My experience mirrored Jesus' because, like Him, I received most of my judgment, hurt, and friction from those who claimed Christ. For Jesus, it was the Pharisees. For me, it was the "saints."

At the end of the day, it was about as comfortable as a spoiled diaper on a baby. It made me itch, and even though I tried to hide it, the smell, or in this case, the essence, seeped right on through. This added another level of beef to the bitterness that I already had towards God, because it seemed like I was labeled "too saved" by both the world and the church. "Pew babies" viewed me as weird just as much, if not more, than my classmates at school. Actually, at times, I was treated with more kindness by the world than the church.

I can share this now with a joyous heart because God has shown me that Jesus' words in Matthew 22:14, "For many are called, but few are chosen," (KJV) was preparation for the fact that chosen and popular are rarely synonymous. Normally, one will suffer while the other is glorified, and as much as I tried to gain popularity, being set apart would not allow it. God's will was going to be done whether I took the original route or some detours instead.

CONFESSIONS OF A PEW BABY (PT. 1)

These detours varied greatly from pressing and pushing to be just like my fellow "pew babies" to saying, "Forget it!" and just accepting that most church youth weren't going to be my friends.

Now, a "pew baby" is an individual who was raised in the church, or better yet, amongst church culture. This typically includes attending Sunday school, staying for the *entire* Sunday morning service, returning for the evening service, participating in the weekly prayer service, coming to Wednesday bible study, tagging along with your mother and father to choir rehearsal and missionary meetings, promoting and attending revivals, participating in fasts and consecrations…you get my drift. The interesting thing to some and strange thing to many is the fact that I actually enjoyed it and found it refreshing.

Unlike the stereotypical pew baby, church was not a chore for me and neither was Christ. Spending time with the Lord was enjoyable because He intrigued me. He was someone I loved learning more about because every new discovery exposed me to power, wisdom, love, kindness, grace, mercy, and Him being I AM that I AM.

Looking at that now, I understand even more why the enemy hit me while I was young. He thought, "I have to catch her now so I can turn the passion she has for Christ to passion towards me. At first she may not realize it is to my aid, but by the time she does, it will be too late." Honestly, that actually may have worked, but I serve a God who will make your detours into training grounds and your stumbling blocks into stepping stones.

However, I did not understand that back then. All those times I read the Bible and studied various biblical figures, from David, to Esther, to Joseph, and even Jesus himself, I had not connected the fact that all of God's chosen went through a period of isolation and were wounded more from those they called friends than those considered foe. So, I was not anticipating the season of seclusion that was to come, but it definitely was waiting.

Like with Job, the enemy was certain that the trials that God was going to allow would break me. What he must have forgotten is that my God is not just wise, He is wisdom, and He would never put more on me than I am able to bear.

Now, I do have to make one thing clear. God had *good* reason to have me face what I did, because even though I was chosen, I was not perfect. There were still chipped, bruised areas which needed correcting,

For example, I had allowed my love for people and my passion for helping morph into a desperate desire for approval. That had to be dealt with and made right, because serving God correctly and wholeheartedly requires for *Christ's* "OK" or will to be your focus. Human's tastes and preferences fluctuate and change more than the temperature throughout the day. No one, kingdom-led or naturally-led, can build a solid foundation on the opinions of others.

This is why God had to put me in a desert season. You see, in another setting, I would ask my neighbor for water if I grew thirsty. However, when I was in the wilderness by myself, I had to depend on the living water to survive, whether I liked it or not.

For some, this still may not make sense because they wonder why God would allow the enemy to use the church as a weapon against me. Looking back at it, though, I see it as an honor and confirmation that the Father has great things for me. Jesus Christ Himself received persecution from the Pharisees, a.k.a. "the church," but He received support from the kingdom, or those who truly gave themselves to God.

This included His disciples, Mary Magdalene, and countless others, and none of them were fancy, title-carrying individuals. They were regular people who had a need and desire for the Lord, and when He filled it, they gave Him their lives as a way of saying, "Thank you!"

Through this taking place in Jesus' life, in the lives of others, and in my life, God was able to further show what He meant in Matthew 13 when He spoke of the wheat and the rare or weeds being allowed to grow together in order to protect the harvest: "'An enemy has done this!' the farmer exclaimed. 'Should we pull out the weeds?' they asked. 'No,' he replied, 'you'll uproot the wheat if you do.'" (Matthew 13:28, 29)

See, the church is similar to a hospital since it is a place for the sick to receive healing. However, none of us are 100% cured or well. We all have ailments that God is healing or strengthening us to overcome. So, no one will witness or should be searching for perfection in the church. What should be sought out and present is obedience, which took me some time to practice and understand myself.

CONFESSIONS OF A PEW BABY (PT. 2)

One part of my struggle with obedience or submission was my refusal to accept the fact that I was not destined to "fit in." A perfect example that I recall is a season where I was striving to blend in more with my classmates. So, I decided to begin cursing when I spoke.

Now, anyone who knows me will vouch for the fact that I am not one to use foul language. Even if I was not a follower of Christ, I still would not use foul language because I feel it is unnecessary. But, I was determined to blend in so that I could belong to something. I did not think about the fact that you cannot do unauthentic things for long if you have real people in your life. Plus, God can use whoever He wishes, whether they are a part of the kingdom or not.

With all of that being said, here is the story. One day in middle school, I was eating lunch with some of my friends and classmates in the cafeteria, and I was using profanity. Now, since my friends used it frequently, I did not think there would be a problem. That's why I was shocked when one of them told me to stop swearing because I didn't even sound right doing it.

First off, I did not see it coming. Second, anyone who knows me will tell you that God has had to deal with me greatly on listening to and taking advice from others, even if they are right. So, I proceeded to tell her how she needed to mind her business, not tell me what to do, etc. We were physically fighting in less than five minutes and both received punishments, mine involving a two-week suspension from school.

Now, this may shock some of you, but as I look back on it, I am very thankful for her honesty. This is one reason why I let it go and we continued our friendship once I returned to school. The truth is necessary whether we like it or not, and the sooner we learn to accept it, regardless of who it is coming from, the better off we will be.

Sadly, I still struggled off and on for many years with this fact. I would have a moment after going to a revival, hearing a quote, or having an encouraging conversation where I would claim that I was ready to accept what God had for me. Then, I would find out that I was not invited to a party or hear someone make a comment about me that I did not like and I would be right back to, "Woe is me." I truly did not understand, or did not want to understand, the difference between being "called" and being "chosen."

According to Dictionary.com, *called* means, "to summon by or as if by divine command," whereas the Oxford Dictionary defines being *chosen* as, "having been selected as the best or most appropriate." Now, I am definitely not bragging or "poppin' my collar," because one must be humble to be in the will of God. My point is simply that when you are the considered the most appropriate individual or are custom-made for the destiny the Lord has for you, then there will be a standard that you have to uphold, as well as differences that will not go away. Regardless of how much you try to hide it or change it, His light will always shine through.

As the Merriam-Webster Dictionary states, *darkness* is when something is, "not receiving, reflecting, transmitting, or radiating light." So, once that light shines through, darkness automatically begins to disappear, and any attempt to bring it back is pointless because the light holds the power.

You want to be on the side where the true power lies. I finally did join that side—God's side—but it was not without trials, bumps, and bruises. Some were set up by the Lord and others were partially or fully self-inflicted by my own hands.

SELF-INFLICTED WOUNDS

Now, before I dig into how that self-inflicted pain occurred, let us look at the meaning behind one simple word: *defense*. According to Dictionary.com, defense is, "resistance against attack or protection." In other words, it means to guard or shield one's self. I did this on a very regular basis by coming for people who I felt came for me.

Since I was small and have never been a fan of fighting, I fought with my tongue. My mouth was quick to run and slow to pause. With that, I began creating a brand that was not all that profitable. I see now that this could have been avoided had I let the Father protect me and stayed in my place.

In 2 Thessalonians 3:3, Paul says, "But the Lord is faithful; he will strengthen you and guard you from the evil one" (NLT). Also, David writes in Psalms, "In peace I will lie down and sleep, for you alone, O Lord, will keep me safe" (Psalms 4:8, NLT). God shows in His Word that He is our shield, but we must believe Him and trust Him for that to abundantly take place.

As a result of His love for us, He still keeps some things away from us. However, other things He will allow us to face so we can gain wisdom and gratefulness, because some of us will not let His wisdom stand due to stubbornness, distrust, bitterness, and other foolishness. Basically, there are times where we must learn the hard way. I know, because I had to learn that way myself.

As a young girl, I was a crowd and church favorite. Except for a few children my age who had issues with me, I was set. Hearing things like, "You're so sweet!", "She's so cute!" and "God has great things for you!" were things I had grown used to, but with life comes change, and the change of moving with my mother did not just bring responsibility. It also introduced me to a growing war that I was not ready for—negative opinions. Now, for those who are wondering how Ms. "I can do all things through Christ" was that affected by others' views, the answer is quite good. I had no training.

Since the majority of the comments I heard about myself were positive, I had no game plan for protecting myself and not letting that negative stuff get to me. So, the various smart remarks hit their target—until I got sick of it and began throwing darts back. That is when things really got interesting because it shifted from acts of defense to direct attacks.

Rather than shielding myself from the people who were intentionally hurting me, I started attacking anyone who appeared to be trying to attack me, and at that time, looking at me wrong felt like an attack. That was when these lips got to flapping and things became ugly, because either I made them feel as small as I did, or they made me feel even worse than I already felt.

At the end of the day, someone was getting hurt, and the only winner was technically Satan, who is already defeated by our Lord and Savior, Jesus Christ. So, why give the devil a free, fake victory? I did not understand that back then, and since I was so determined to "win" every unpleasant encounter, I developed a strategy. Instead of only attacking someone whenever I felt attacked, which was about 99.99% of the time, I also began having a response prepared whenever I had a conversation.

Now, some people may say, "That's not bad. It just keeps you from getting pushed around." I do give credit to those people for coming up with a logical analysis of the situation. The only problem is that, at that time, I was not thinking of a wise or mature way to handle the situation. My mind was chilling and my emotions were in full control of my response. Basically, since *Amber* was worried about if *Amber's* points would be made so that *Amber's* voice was heard, *Amber* was going to plan her response while others were talking to her. It was all about Amber.

This resulted in not having time to "waste" listening to another person's point of view. My goal was to make sure that I was heard and agreed with. Some may not see that as a problem, but for me, a young woman who says she serves an unselfish God who I am striving to be more like, I was completely going in the opposite direction.

Rather than taking the time and being mature enough to show the vulnerability necessary to care about others, Amber was caring about Amber. She had good intentions, and was trying to fill a void she had, but only one person could fill that space—God.

So, as time went on, my defensive attitude continued to grow. The people who cared for me tried their very best to share with me that while I thought was protecting my heart, I was actually breaking the hearts of others and damaging mine by pushing people away. This truly stung because I am a true "people person." God made me that way for His purpose in my life. Thankfully, as I look back, I see that the Lord used my actions and the results as a way to purify me and teach me lessons that I can now share with others.

Amazingly, by the hand of God, I still had people in my life who were my friends and mentors who became just like family as the years went on. Even they had to look past my tough exterior, which included my smart mouth, swift comebacks, and "interesting" relationship with my mother. They did not excuse my actions or agree with them, and they made that clear to me. Seeing behind the mask that I put and tried to keep on did, however, show them where the seeds to the weeds were.

This led them to try to help me destroy the seeds and pluck up the weeds in my life. That way, not only would they be removed, but what was intended to grow would be destroyed or put under spiritual authority. Unfortunately, there was one thing making this more difficult than it had to be, and that was my disinterest in getting answers and requesting guidance from God, the head gardener.

You see, He knows me better than I know myself because He made me. My life, from beginning to end, is known by Him and was laid by Him, and His will *will* be done. As Proverbs 19:21 says, "You can make plans, but the Lord's purpose will prevail" (NLT). Seeking Him for the answers is the only way to get a true solution. However, when you have "beef" or negative feelings against someone, you most likely are not going to seek their counsel and direction, even when they are in control.

Thankfully, I have learned that and I have to remind myself of it, especially when the independent part of my personality kicks in. Back then, however, I had not trained my flesh to recognize and submit with the help of God. This not only affected my relationship with God and others, such as my spiritual and natural family, but it also caused a gap to grow between someone else important in my life: my mother.

R-E-S-P-I-C-T

"R-E-S-P-E-C-T. Find out what it means to me. R-E-S-P-E-C-T. Take care, TCB." Many of us who love a good, classic song and know parts of our entertainment culture are familiar with the song that include the lyrics above. We also are very familiar with the main topic of the song: respect. This seven-letter word carries various layers and aspects that show us strengths that should be maintained and weaknesses that need to be eliminated.

With these various layers, aspects, and encounters come different interpretations. According to Dictionary.com, *respect* means to have, "esteem for or a sense of the worth or excellence of a person…." For some, keeping the definition of respect on one accord with how we actually feel is simple. However, for me, it was a bit more complicated due to the fact that it required me to let things go and move forward, which I honestly did not want to do at the time.

For me, respect and forgiveness were cousins I did not want to reunite. The thought of having to "let go" of so much and show respect to someone I wanted to remind of their mistakes made me mad and frustrated. However, I needed, and I do mean needed, to allow God to teach me about respect because I was using all of this as an excuse and reason to disrespect my mother. I felt I did not owe her anything and that she gotten more than she deserved from me.

In my opinion, if anyone in our home needed to be shown respect and gratitude, it was me. The fact that most of the time I cared for my mother on my own was: A) something I felt I should be praised or "given props" for; and B) another part of my life that I added to my list of grudges against God.

What I failed to remember was that God knows best, and like any good father, He will not lead us to be overwhelmed. He knows what every one of us can handle and will not allow any trials or tribulations to overtake us. Many times, He must either prove to us what we can endure or remind us that He is always by our side. However, at the time, I was sick of being strong because, to me, the benefits did not outweigh the responsibilities.

Truthfully, I felt having endurance was no longer worth it and being "chosen" was not all it was cracked up to be. I cannot speak for everyone else, but I was not thinking of the fact that just like the natural strength in our physical bodies is developed by lifting weights and working out, one's spiritual strength is developed the same way. The weights may vary from frustration, loneliness, disappointment and other struggles, but the goal is always to allow you to see what God sees and for that potential to become a reality.

Whether it is a strength that you hold or a weakness that you possess, experience is one of God's greatest tools. Not only will you grow through the test, but you will also be able to aid others. Sadly, everyone does not and will not see this as a positive thing, because it means they are suffering on someone else's behalf. That requires a spirit of selflessness that is not easy for everyone to acquire. I myself have to press for the spirit of selflessness, not selfishness, to be in control. Looking back on that time, though, my concerns were basically "me, myself, and I".

Unfortunately, this manifested greatly in how I treated my mother. Between my bitterness toward God and my unforgiveness towards my father, I had an enormous amount of pent up anger, and it was released on the main person around me: my mom. Now, I was upset with her about some of her choices, but rather than that being the sole source of the frustration I expressed, there were various other things fueling that fire.

So, here I was, a young, church-going girl who was pissed with more believers than unbelievers and who had put aside respecting her mother for her own personal feelings. Not only that, but rather than being hit by daily conviction and trying in some way to correct myself, I typically tried to justify my actions.

That is one thing about being intelligent and feeling entitled. Without even recognizing it, you may start making excuses regarding almost any and every thing you do. Scriptures such as, "And you shall know the truth, and the truth shall make you free," (John 8:32, NKJV) at that time were going on the back burner and ones like, "But if there is further injury, the punishment must match the injury: a life for a life, an eye for an eye, a tooth for a tooth, a hand for a hand, a foot for a foot," (Exodus 21:23-24, NLT) were my main focus.

I felt that every smart comment, eye roll, disobedient moment, and disrespectful act was a result of my mom's (and father's and God's) decisions. What I failed to realize at the time was that neither she nor my dad could control God's plan for my life. All they could do was play their roles in it. I did not understand, or to be brutally honest, I didn't want to understand, that for something to reach its value there must be cleansing, shaping, and polishing.

Any piece of amber is beautiful, but I doubt many consumers would want to wear it in a piece of jewelry if there has been no cleaning and upkeep. Personally, I did not like God's process for this jewel, but as Isaiah 55:8 says, "For my thoughts are not your thoughts, neither are your ways my ways, saith the LORD" (KJV), and as Proverbs 3:5 states, "Trust in the LORD with all thine heart; and lean not unto thine own understanding" (KJV).

Thankfully, I have progressed (even though I am not perfect) in this area since then. This is why I can tell you, without a shadow of a doubt, that I did not want to hear that, let alone follow it at the time. Why? That answer is simple, yet pointless. I wanted to be in control.

Since I thought I knew everything and could decipher what was best, I subconsciously and consciously began to always desire to have the "say so." This started regarding God and my life and trickled down to one of the individuals He chose to use to birth me: my mother.

Due to having little shame regarding my behavior back then, I hid this from no one. I was blunt and a bit proud with my actions. This led to many, especially Christians, seeing my disrespectful behavior. I myself did not see much of a problem with it, until people began following simple, yet strong advice: "If someone shows you who they are, believe them." This resulted in a mark on me that would truly take washing with the living water to fade.

BAD BRANDING

Now, if I were to ask a room full of people, "What is a brand?" I believe a lot of people would say it is a line of clothing, food, services, etc. If I then requested examples, some might say Coca-Cola. Others may answer Coach. Some around my age may even name Uber or Snapchat. However, Dictionary.com lists, "a kind or variety of something distinguished by some distinctive characteristic," as another definition for brand. You also have Thesaurus.com giving, "type, kind," as the first definition, and, "cast, character, class," are the first of various synonyms listed.

So, as you can see, "brand" can easily be referring to the soda you are sipping on as well as the attitude you have while drinking that Coke (or Pepsi for some people, including myself). This I learned up close and personal, because the various words that came out my mouth without restraint or discipline began creating a brand that would be very difficult to change in the future. As they say, the first impression is key, and I had left enough first impressions to last a lifetime.

Ironically enough, my behavior was a reaction to receiving negative treatment and being isolated, and in the end, it led to receiving even more of those same things. Improperly addressing a tree's root allows it to grow, and no matter how many leaves and branches you snatch off, if you do not face the roots, you are wasting your time.

Thankfully, as I mentioned earlier, there were some who looked past my "brand" and took a look at the ingredients. Two of those families were the Drew and the Grace families. They are two families I will never forget because they loved me when I did not even know what love was.

The Drew family includes Brother Lewis Drew, a.k.a. "Uncle Lewis", Sister Brenda Drew, a.k.a. "Aunt Brenda," Amanda White, Ken, and Van. I met this family while I was a member of my home church, where Uncle Lewis is a deacon. One Sunday, from what I remember, my mother and I were invited to their home for dinner. This led me on a full discovery of the kindness, care, and love in their hearts. After that, the rest is history.

The closeness that developed between us was truly a blessing from God above. We laughed, talked, shared, and I even accepted moments of correction. We developed such a strong bond that Amanda even began calling my mom "Auntie," which led to me calling her parents Uncle Lewis and Aunt Brenda. They went from fellow church members to 100% family in the spiritual and the emotional realm, and this family took a chance on me by letting me into their hearts. For doing that, I will forever be grateful for them.

Due to God's grace and mercy, I not only experienced this kingdom affection with the Drew's. The door of love was also opened by the Grace's. The leader of this family unit, Sister Sandra Grace, was serving in the military at the time, which led her and her children to move to Virginia a few years after my mother and I returned.

Now, I cannot say I remember exactly what my first "up-close and personal" interaction was with Sister Grace, but I will say that I am grateful that she looked past my outbursts, ignored possible hearsay, and decided to give me a chance. As a result of the brand I had made for myself and my behavior when things did not go my way, she had every right to avoid me. However, she took a leap of faith, leading to a relationship that has yet to end.

From conversations where I was praised for my accomplishments to times where I was corrected for rude outbursts, she kept it real with me. I am forever grateful for these two examples and others who God used to invest in me at a time where I did not recognize my own value. It was a true blessing, and I will never forget it.

As the time and the years went on, my appreciation for those blessings from God remained, but it only showed to a certain extent. You see, the love I received from these families and others would briefly brighten my soul, but because I had not fully attempted to identify and snatch up the root of the problem, the fruit remained the same. As Matthew 7:16 says, "You can identify them by their fruit, that is, by the way they act" (Matthew 7:16A, NLT).

So, my brand continued to become a darker and darker shade of red with a sign that read, "Beware." Of course, those who knew what was really behind all of that hung in there with me, but others decided to keep their distance. This basically continued for years, all the way into 2011. By then, God had granted my wish of being asked to join the praise team at my church, which was a chance on the leader's side and a time of necessary growth for me because it required me keeping my emotions and reactions in check. There was no room for explosions out of frustration.

However, it was very much worth it because it allowed my love for singing to be used to praise and worship the God who granted the gift to me. It gave me a taste of what it felt like to use my abilities to the glory of the Lord. So, I did what I had to do—in some areas.

My mother's seizure activity during the summer of 2010 had become more frequent. Due to not walking in much natural or spiritual maturity at that time, I reacted to it in a very unwise way. I basically just decided to tell life, "Forget You!" I began practicing extreme truancy, which is the action of "staying away from school without good reason," during the 2010-2011 school year.

In the beginning, I would say that I was not feeling well. As time went on, though, I grew so bold with it that I just began saying that I was not going. It got so bad that, twice, my mother had to call the cops to get me to go. However, this was only known by a few members of my spiritual family.

During this time, I was acting a fool and still attempting to show God glory through song. The only thing with that is, it's impossible. Hebrews 13:8 clearly states, "Jesus Christ is the same yesterday, today, and forever" (NLT). If we are going to live as our Father in heaven would live, then there can be no switching up, sneaking, or hiding.

That is why the wake-up call that God sent me was so powerful. It had to bring me out of hiding and cause me to address my life's negative roots while appreciating where God had me. Thankfully, it did all of that and then some, making me come out of my ungodly sleep and take the first step into the change God had for me, one alarm at a time.

WAKE-UP CALL (PT. 1)

In 2010, *Time Magazine* released a piece online by Alice Park titled, "Study: How Our Brains Make Us Light or Heavy Sleepers." This particular article touched on what causes some to be able to sleep through surrounding disturbances better than others and how, "scientists...identified and measured the process."

Dr. Jeffrey Ellenbogen, the neurologist and leader of the study, along with the sleep researchers at Harvard Medical School and Massachusetts General Hospital, decided to discover and test if the answer to the difference came from a place rarely considered. In the words of Ellenbogen, "I'm adding a third perspective - the brain. Because the key part of normal healthy sleep is being able to block the response to sounds."

During this study, Ellenbogen discovered that the difference likely was due to the amount of pulses or sleep spindles per person. According to his findings, those with more spindles slept through more disruptions and those with less spindles could sleep through less.

It was a new finding, but Ellenbogen was confident the discovery would help others sleep better. As he said, "...we need to figure out how to block that sound from getting the brain to cause you to wake." In layman's terms, whoever shuts things out best, sleeps longer. This is something I know to be true, but in a slightly different fashion. But that will get touched on later.

So, the year is 2011 and the month is August. Summer is wrapping up, and my truancy has had a domino effect on my academic life, causing my GPA to go from above a 3.0 to a 2.52. As a result, I had to leave the Pre-IB (International Baccalaureate) Program at Warwick High School and transfer to Heritage High School.

With all of the above and more taking place, it is clear why my mother and I were very excited when a church friend invited us to join her and her son on a trip to Nashville, Tennessee to visit a family member. A time of travel, fun, and refreshment sounded lovely. Plus, being a music lover and singer, I was beyond excited because Nashville would expose me to a side of the industry I had not seen before. Basically, the list of the trip's benefits spoke for itself. So we decided to take a break and go.

During the apparent 10 hours and 8 minutes it takes to get from Newport News, Virginia to Nashville, Tennessee, we talked, laughed, even viewed a cool tree and sign or two. Before we knew it, we were saying hello to Nashville and stepping into a season that no one knew was coming.

While in Nashville, we stayed with our friend's mother. We were able to visit a church the friend knew well and had attended often. We were even able to find out about some history as well.

Unfortunately, even though I had slightly changed my behavior due to switching schools, I still did not value my mother and recognize her true worth in my life. This resulted in some "hidden" arguments and disagreements. In my opinion at the time, things were not going that bad. We were ok, until about a day or two before we were set to go home. That's when the alarm began to sound.

So, according to my mother, she was concerned about us traveling to a different climate and whether it would have a negative effect on her body, causing her to have seizures. Because of this, she received prayer from her current and my previous pastor before we went on the road. However, as we all know, if something is in God's plan, there is no avoiding it.

My mother's seizures were in His because she did, which led us to check her into a Tennessee hospital. This lasted for a couple of days and once she was well, they released her and we hit the road with our friend and headed back to Newport News, Virginia. We all thought this chapter was ending. Little did we know, this was only the beginning.

Once we got into the car, we began to rest and prepare for the hours of driving ahead. However, I quickly noticed that things were not right with my mother. Our friend also began to notice, and we could tell there would not be a smooth road ahead. My mother began having seizures again while we were on the road. Since we were not able to predict her movements during the episodes, we decided to move her to the backseat for safety.

Thankfully, with the friend and I both having humorous personalities, there were plenty of laughs and giggles during the ride. Her presence helped greatly and truly showed what the elders meant when they said, "Laugh to keep from crying." The lightness of her soul and true joy she possessed helped me to not dwell on what was taking place with my mother and leave it in God's hands for a short period of time. I did not know it at that time, but I would be putting even more in the Father's hands really soon.

That morning, after hours of open road, music, and fellowship, we finally all reached Virginia, and my mother and I made it home. As we all parted, we hoped that with some rest and the crazy faith my mother possessed, her health and body would return to normal. Due to my issues with God at the time, the thought never crossed my mind to pray for strength even if God had different plans.

As the day went on, the seizures did not cease, and my level of worry increased with every single one that took place. In spite of the tension that my home had endured and the disrespect I had shown, I still loved her. Under all of the "I don't care!" "You get on my nerves!" kicking, screaming, and back talk was a little girl who did not want her mother to leave her side.

So, I ended up calling 9-1-1 and we headed to the hospital. Through "word of mouth" and some phone calls, others who were close to us found out and word began to spread. There were probably enough prayers going up to cover an apartment, and I was thankful for them. However, one thing I have learned since then is that prayer is a conversation with God and there is a chance that He will say, "No."

As time went on, things did not improve and my mother was moved from the emergency room to a room for an extended stay. While there, the repeated seizures began mixing with short, unidentifiable spats. Sometimes her eyes would remain open during the spat while the machine that was attached to her would begin making numerous noises. Other times, she would quickly sit-up with her body super tight, staring forward. It was as if her body was on its own random agenda.

So, I sat there, watching television, listening to music, and giving people updates on how she was. I pretty much did anything that would help distract me from what was actually going on and who I actually needed to get through it. Even though I needed God more than ever at this time, I still had not allowed myself to be fully vulnerable and true with Him. I still was not awake.

By our third day, the doctors discovered that the machine's noises and jumps, as well as my mother swiftly sitting up and jerking, were also signs of seizures. This meant that my mother actually had an enormously larger amount of episodes than we all thought. This caused other issues to come into play. Even a stroke was becoming a concern as a result of her physical state. So, the doctors decided to basically medicate her into a coma to protect her and prevent this from taking place.

Now, one meaning of *awake* is actually, "to come or bring to an awareness or to become cognizant." It was around this time that the above definition began manifesting in my life. I am going to be honest. I did try to hit the snooze button, because I did not want to acknowledge what I was about to walk into. However, the seeds I had planted could not be ignored and the fruit they were about to bring forth was not going to be pretty.

WAKE-UP CALL (PT. 2)

As the seconds, minutes, and hours went by, things began to become more and more complicated. Not only were the seeds that I planted bringing forth unpleasant fruit, but the vines were getting tangled up in the process. I could no longer hit the snooze button because the alarms were sounding more than ever.

Due to my mother's condition, we were informed that she would have to be placed on a liquid diet for a time to gradually get her body used to doing everyday things like eating. She would have to be cared for for a time, starting with a short time in a rehabilitation center.

According to the doctors, it would take anywhere from six to twelve months for this process to be completed. Not only did this shock my family, but it left tough decisions to have to be made. One was, who would take care of my mother? Another was, who would take care of me?

Now, there is an old saying that goes, "You are free to choose, but you are not free from the consequence of your choice." I definitely learned this during this time, because due to my behavior over the years, including my issues with truancy, not much of my family wanted to take me on as a responsibility. The brand I had created for myself was finally bringing forth major results, and they were not what I had expected, but they were accurate.

Looking back at it, I can truly see what the elders or older generation in our lives mean when they say, "You're a child. You don't know any better." I behaved that way because I was not happy with how my life was going, not considering that my actions would not better things if life took a turn. Well, whether I thought about it or not, it was happening and it woke me up like never before.

I no longer could "block...the sounds" as Ellenbogen discussed. These events were to me what the captain was to Jonah when he said, "'How can you sleep at a time like this?'... 'Get up and pray to your god!'" (Jonah 1:6, NLT) With all that was going on, I did, too, because I had nothing to lose and everything to gain.

I remember it like it was yesterday. My mother was in her hospital room, still unconscious from the medication. As I looked at her, I felt tears coming down my face as a myriad of emotions ran through my mind.

With the way things had been going, I had no idea what the future held or if my mother would be in it. So, I prayed a very simple, gut-wrenching prayer. I said, "Lord, if my mother dies, help me to still serve You." I knew that would be her dying wish and with all that I had put her through, it was the least I could do if God took her home.

Being a teenager at the time, I did not realize that God was moving in the situation, using it for good. The fact that my prayer mirrored the selflessness Christ showed in the Garden of Gethsemane when He prayed that God's will be done (Matthew 26:39) was a leap that I did not even realize I was taking. Slowly but surely, I was recognizing it was not all about me. This, along with support from God, helped me through this time of mild chaos and major consequences.

One tool that the Father used to lift my spirit was some of my spiritual family who called regarding my mother, visited the hospital, and offered words of encouragement. Sister Grace even took me out to eat and requested I spend the weekend with her as a "mini-vacation." The love shown through this, along with the edification from worship music and musical testimonies, helped pull me through.

I cannot tell you how many times I listened to "Best in Me" by Marvin Sapp to lift my spirits, and it did just that. The thought that God still loved me in spite of what I had done and how I had acted truly touched my heart. That, along with the idea that He still saw worth in me, helped me to go on.

As days went by and multiple conversations took place, I began to realize that there was no avoiding having to leave my home for a while. So, I stopped arguing with my local family and agreed to go live with my father.

I called and talked to him about it. For various reasons, he was unsure about it. This led me to recommend to my grandmother that she speak to my stepmother about the matter. With the help of that conversation, they were able to come to an agreement that I would stay in Alabama with my father and stepmother until my mother fully recovered.

Now, I would be lying out the side of my mouth if I said that I wanted to leave, because I absolutely did not. However, debating with my family was not going to help anything. I had to simply put my hands up and surrender. Was I happy about it? No. Did God use it to work in my life? Yes.

One major thing that I began learning firsthand was selflessness, which I mentioned earlier. You see, through grace and favor, my mother did become conscious before I left town, and some were concerned about how she would respond to my leaving, especially without her final stamp of approval.

So, I was told that I could not share with her that I was temporarily moving away during her recovery. I was unhappy about that. However, in this life, there is no way to truly avoid anything. At home, I did not want to be obedient when my mother commanded things timidly, and with all that was going on, I had to follow commands that were presented much differently.

As a result, I visited my mother after Sunday service with a fellow saint. She did not know this, but it would be the last time we saw each other for a little while. Thankfully, she and I both serve a God who is in control.

With the Father taking the wheel and me not having any other options but to command my soul to trust Him, I prepared myself for the move. My grandmother happened to have a friend who was traveling to a nearby community, which was a connection that was right on time.

So, I was quickly heading to a new state to add an additional road to my journey. Truthfully, at the time, I did not know if it was a new beginning or just an unexpected detour. All I knew was that I had to trust God—no matter what the cost. This required stepping out of denial and attempting to step into truth with a person who I doubted would ever step into it with me: my father.

REUNION

According to Dictionary.com, the formal definition of *closure* is, "a bringing to an end" or "conclusion." Basically, it means to cease or end something. When I've heard others use the term, the connotation or feeling is a bit different. People are normally discussing finding out why something happened or why someone did something. It is all about the answers, and without realizing it, one can make it all about oneself.

When I went to live with my father in August 2011 due to my mother's health issues, I did not know it, but, subconsciously, that was one of the things I wanted. Of course, being that it had been six years since I saw my father, I honestly had no idea what to expect.

Some may not understand how confusing this may be, but it is harder than some may think. This was someone I used to spend almost all day and every day with. People who knew us both would always tell me how much we acted alike. I was even told when I was younger that I looked like him, and ironically, by this time, I sometimes struggled to remember what he looked like.

That is why, rather than being excited about the situation, I was worried and afraid. The worry was for my mother and her health. The fear was rooted in not knowing if my father and I were a lost cause or if we would be able to pick up where we left off.

Now, my grandmother's friend telling me that my leaving Virginia was not an easy decision for my grandmother comforted me a bit, because it helped me battle the feeling of abandonment by showing me that there still was some form of love and care between us.

However, the other two emotions that I previously mentioned did not instantly go away. I felt like I had no control, and I hated it. The closer we got to the house, the less I felt like I was at the steering wheel of life. It was almost like there was a giant hand shoving me in a direction I did not want to go. Thankfully, I now recognize it was God the Father guiding me, so I would not fall.

As we pulled up to the house and I stepped out of the car, it was as if a ghost was standing there greeting me. The very thing I had wanted, no, begged God for, I was getting, but the fact that I was not receiving it how I had planned ate at my soul. So, as my father stood in front of me, and I was told by one of the adults on the scene to give him a hug, I realized that I had no idea what I was walking into. I also no longer knew if I should be angry with God for keeping us separate or appreciate the fact that He was doing what was best.

Now, it is not that I do not love my father, but even people who love each other sometimes need time apart. Plus, you cannot force someone to change or see things from your perspective. All you can do is do or say what God has assigned for you in their journey. As 1 Corinthians 3:7 states, "So then neither is he that planteth any thing, neither he that watereth;

but God that giveth the increase" (KJV). Several times, I had attempted to rush God, and now that it seemed like He was going with my time, I had no idea what to think.

With every second that passed, I began to understand what those who were wiser than me meant when they said, "Be careful what you wish for." My wish was coming true, and I felt like it was becoming a reality too soon.

However, these were the cards I had been dealt, and the only choice I had was to do my best to play my hand well. So, I went in with my things and met my stepmother and stepsister who also lived in the house. The sweet, kind nature of them both helped to break the ice and shatter some of my worry.

Since this was the first time I had lived with my father in six years and the first time I had lived with my blended family, period, I was nervous. I soon discovered that I was not the only one who was worried about how this would all turn out.

See, everyone deals with life differently. Some shop to make themselves feel better. Others watch a television show or two to ease their spirits. There are even a few individuals who use smartphones to drain the pain away.

From what I have seen, my father's stress reliever was alcohol. It allowed him to calm himself and clear his mind. In many ways, it had become his pain killer. Unfortunately, this relief was always artificial. Once the buzz disappeared and life was back in full focus, the issues had not gone away.

My hope was that by this time he would have developed a new escape. That maybe music would solely have the lead role. Maybe even that God had been allowed to step into that position, which is rightfully His. But when I caught a whiff of alcohol on my father, my intuition told me that booze still was in that place.

Like many women, I told myself that I was wrong and that I should not make assumptions. However, he stepped into honesty that night, which I greatly respect, admitting that he was nervous about our living together and had drank to muffle that. Now, I hoped that this would not be a regular occurrence, but even God Himself offers free will. If the Great I AM does not force others to do what He wants, I definitely cannot.

As time went on and things began falling into a routine involving school and life, it seemed as if everything may work out ok. I spoke to my mother and friends in Virginia, which helped ease my mind and bring temporary peace, and I fell into place at school by joining choir, trying to adjust to class, and working on my social life.

Plus, by the grace of God, my mother was recovering quicker than planned. The only real issue was that birds of a feather were finding it hard to flock together. In other words, my father and I were not getting along.

Number one, we both have extremely strong personalities and enjoy speaking our minds. Also, even though I knew that the Bible says, "Honor thy father and mother," I struggled with it because my father had not really been there in a while.

Now, we spoke on the phone during the six years that we were apart, but there was no face-to-face contact. Between the questions I had for my father and the distance that I had developed from him and God, I began to feel like giving him respect was a benefit, not a necessity.

Deciding if you will or you won't do things based on your feelings will get you nowhere. You must do the right thing regardless of what anyone else is or is not doing. There is no way you can plant sour seeds and reap sweet fruit.

Unfortunately, it was not just that that caused friction. Expectations played a big part too. You see, I expected for things to be very simple. In my mind I would just move in, talk to my father about him and my mother's marriage, get some answers, and move on. My father expected for me to come to Alabama, move in, and stay two years until I graduated from high school. As you may have guessed, neither of us got what we wanted.

When I approached my father about the physical violence that took place between him and my mother, I was told that he was not responsible. By the end of the conversation, I was being told that I had been fed all of this by different family members.

Now, my motive for having this talk with him was merely to get answers and closure. That way, we both could move forward in our father-daughter relationship. So, the fact that it was appearing to become a "blame game" baffled me.

First, since most of the dysfunction between my parents occurred behind closed doors, there was no way I could have been convinced that it happened because I was the main witness.

Plus, as a result of my mother experiencing seizures, she does not remember as much as I do when it comes to that. She views that as a blessing in disguise and uses it as one of her tools to praise God in spite of.

So, with the above encounter going badly, there was definitely tension in the air. I was not going to get what I wanted in that area. Then, as God began having His way even more and blowing all of our minds, things got stirred up even more.

Back in my home state, Virginia, my mother's recovery was breaking all of the estimates. According to what I was being told, she would be fully recovered in approximately three months, which was a quarter of the time that the doctor initially estimated. However, shifting time also shifts schedules and hopes, and that changes things up.

This truly showed when I spoke to my father about my mother's rapid improvement. At first, everything seemed like it was good. Then, I mentioned leaving Alabama and going home sooner than originally planned. That's when things got interesting.

My father was expecting me to stay longer—much longer. His hope was that I would stay for two years, until I graduated from high school. The only problem with that was that Virginia was my home.

My leaving was not out of excitement. It was purely out of emergency. I was not communicating with God as I should have been at that time, but I knew that being there was only for a season, and how long that season would be was being determined by God's healing power.

My father wanting a second chance with me was great because it showed that I still mattered, which is something I had questioned, but I knew it happening that way was not God's will. I loved my father, but I was not going to force myself to remain in a temporary situation for a long period of time. My love for him was not going to surpass my desire to do what was right and what was God.

So, I told him that I was not going to stay longer than I had to, and that wreaked havoc. We went from having a small, simple disagreement here and there to arguing multiple times a week. Plus, with his anger during the previous clashes already reaching a high level, you can imagine the feeling of rejection he felt. And the alcohol he used to soothe it did not help.

It almost felt like I had been slapped into my mother's old shoes. My stepsister supported me greatly with conversation and company, but the only reason I got through was God Himself, because my heart and soul felt like a mess. Between going straight to my room after calling my mother when I got home from school to losing most of my appetite, I was knocking on the door of depression. However, God's comfort and love kept me, giving me the strength to press towards the finish line.

As weeks went on, the tension in the house continued to grow. I spoke to my mother, my grandmother, and even a local youth minister about the situation. Everyone said the same thing.

Since there was no transfer of legal custody, I did not have to stay with my father. Now, I did not have any money at the time to fund my leaving, but that bit of hope helped me greatly. Also, God decided to show out because my mother called me not long after saying that a church member was going to purchase my plane ticket back to Virginia.

Now, my father was not pleased, and it caused an even deeper riff between us for some months, but God was moving greatly and who was I to tell Him, "No!" So, I did what was necessary to get the ticket, got my stepsister to take me to the airport, and headed back home to Newport News, Virginia.

Of course, I knew that relationships in Alabama and Virginia required repair. With all of the twists and turns I had recently experienced, I had begun to see that even though important things were not always comfortable, they were necessary—and worth it.

CALLED TO CHANGE

You know, change is an amazing thing. Sometimes it can be drastic. Other times it can be subtle. Plus, you cannot always determine what will fuel its launch. There is actually a quote by Richelle E. Goodrich that says, "It isn't always a change of scenery needed to make life better. Sometimes it simply requires opening your eyes."

This is so true, because it was not simply being in Alabama that caused me to work towards changing my life. Having to imagine life without the blessings (my mother, home, and friends) that God had given me opened my eyes. I got to see things without rose-colored glasses and it showed me the truth. This led me to realize that change had to start with me.

By coming to this realization, I developed a good foundation, but I still had details to work on. This left many possible "if's," "and's," or "but's," because starting over requires a new plan and a fresh fire. Also, a revitalization like this needs two more central things: faith and dedication.

Now, these honestly had been areas where I had previously struggled, which is why I thank God that His desire from us is to surrender, not to be perfect. Still, I am someone who finds it easy to fall into routine.

Because of this, readjusting and breaking habits are not strong points for me, even if the change is for my good. This is another area in which God-ordained help from the outside showed up and showed out. The Father used people from before and also added a new team member to the mix. Her name is Alicia Stewart.

As a result of the Warwick High truancy issue that I mentioned earlier, I was scheduled to transfer to Heritage High School at the start of my junior year, and this did not change because I left for a little while. So, when I returned, I had to adjust to a new environment and setting.

Thankfully, God gave me a little comfort since I went to Crittenden Middle School with over half of Heritage High's student body. Now, people may change after two years, especially during their teenage years, but the fact that I knew them already did give me a bit of a head start.

Another thing that brought me some comfort during this time of transition was joining the school choir. Being able to use the voice God gave me was an amazing, fun outlet. The only issue was that I was still having a slight problem with truancy due to struggling with laziness and not being a morning person. However, God knew exactly who to have me under at school to nip that right in the bud.

It all started around Christmas 2011. I had been singing alto in the beginner's choir for about three months, and my love for Christmas and singing was strong as ever. Plus, with a concert at the school coming up, I was bubbling with energy and happiness. That happiness and energy decided to go from high to higher when the teacher's assistant recommended to Mrs. Stewart, the choir director, that I audition for one of the solos.

There is an old saying that I have heard numerous times, and it still holds power to this day. It states, "It takes a village to raise a child." I learned quickly that this was something Mrs. Stewart truly lives by, because she went straight into "mom-mode" in this situation.

The minute the teacher's assistant suggested my auditioning for a solo, she said, "I ain't having no one sing who can't come to school." I was so shocked that I fell into silence. Now, I see that it was preparation for the future.

Even the Bible says, "When someone has been given much, much will be required in return; and when someone has been entrusted with much, even more will be required" (Luke 12:48, NLT).

My wanting glory from something without desiring to take on the responsibility that comes with it has been a weakness that I have struggled with for years. So, her putting her foot down was necessary and appreciated. It made such a difference that less than a few months later, I approached her and said, "Thank you!" because even though it did not give me what I wanted, it gave me what I needed. Hearing those words helped me to push harder, and had I not heard them, I have no idea how certain things would have played out.

As the school year went on, I was able to work on improving my attendance, which became better over time. This allowed my voice to be used freely in the choir, and my gift was not returned unto me void, because I was able to use my gift of song to honor God. A perfect example of that was my very first solo at Heritage High School.

It was the spring of 2012 and Heritage's annual gospel concert was right around the corner. I was beyond excited because I love good music, especially when it is praising and worshipping the God I serve. However, my excitement wound up mixing with nervousness when Mrs. Stewart told me that I would be singing lead on a song by the beginner's choir. That slight anxiousness grew even more when I was as informed that the song was being changed from "Holy Is The Lamb" by Oleta Adams to "Yes" by Shekinah Glory.

Now, neither of these songs are simple, and both are well-known. However, among the people I know personally who have made a difference in my life, "Yes" is a priceless ode of worship. You do not sing that song without skill, and more importantly, you do not just sing. You minister.

This led to rehearsals with the choir, private rehearsals at home, and even looking closer at my walk with God. They say you have to practice what you preach, and I feel that includes what you sing, too. Thankfully, doing this created a double blessing. At the time, my home life was "interesting," and that particular song encouraged me tremendously. So, the process leading up to my ministering to others ministered to me as well.

By the time the concert came, I felt pretty vocally prepared, but spiritually I was not where I needed to be. Awesomely, I experienced an amazing spiritual release at a Sunday morning service that day that gave me a taste of freedom that was truly necessary. Once I got to Heritage later that day, I was able to use my gift with joy, peace, and anointing like never before.

The privilege of being able to sing and minister a song that speaks on submission, trust, faith, obedience, purpose, and destiny is something that you never forget. Every time I remember that not only was I able to edify or encourage others, but myself also, I am beyond grateful, because it was not about pleasing others. The goal was to please God, and it was reached. I am very thankful that that goal was reached, because the season I had just stepped into was going to require positive memories of days like that, as well as support from others and unmatchable love from God. There were going to be blessings, but they would not be reached easily. Like the saints say, "If He brings you to it, He'll bring you through it," and life was about to give me an advanced lesson.

VICTORIES IN THE VALLEY

Now, according to statistics, there were 1,360,747 homeless public-school students in the 2013-2014 school year, and 18,486 of these pupils lived in Virginia. By the time that data was collected, I was a college freshman at a private university, but I was still homeless.

That situation is something I will never forget because of the strength it brought me and lessons it taught me. Though I had already experienced it before, that time was truly the season that I consider most interesting and unique. It all started in 2012.

March was already here, and my mother had been unemployed for about a year. She'd been receiving unemployment during that time, but due to confusion and chaos during her rehabilitation and recovery, she had not reapplied. This resulted in that money no longer coming and us having to say good-bye to our apartment.

We moved in with my grandmother for the remainder of my junior year in high school. That following summer, we lived in a couple of places, including a building specifically for single mothers and their children. By the beginning of fall, we were living in a hotel.

Those in our lives did offer their support in various ways. Even on my first day of school, Mrs. Stewart gave me a ride to school, since I had no idea what bus to catch. However, it was still a wilderness season. By the time the winter came, my mother and I were living in a shelter program which involved us moving from church to church every week.

This resulted in numerous school bus stops and rides on the local city buses with suitcases full of stuff. Also, since I sang in two of Heritage High's vocal ensembles, I spent many days carpooling to and from school with Mrs. Stewart and even some nights sleeping at her house.

As time went on and we bounced around from place to place, the places that I called "home" began to add up. Over a three-month period, I slept in at least 12 churches. This required many moments of belief and faith. Honestly, I was not very strong in heart at the time, but my mouth was. Due to this, various backroads and pieces of luggage got to witness my frustration firsthand. Unfortunately, that frustration was directly taken out on my mother.

See, at the time, I did not realize that this was necessary for the move God was about to do in my life. It was unfair punishment, not required preparation. Thankfully, I had a mother who loved me despite my behavior and a God who showed favor in spite of my lack of faith.

I know this because she continued to treat me with care and tenderness, and the Father continued to keep me and began passing out blessings that I did not even see coming. The first one that really shocked me was meeting and singing for the 44th President and First Lady of the United States of America, Barack and Michelle Obama.

I remember it like it was yesterday. It was December 2012 and the Christmas season had already begun. Now, anyone who is close to me knows that Christmas is my favorite holiday. Being a believer, celebrating Jesus Christ's birth is an honor.

Also, I love the commercial aspects of the season. Whether it is singing Christmas carols, drinking eggnog, watching holiday movies, or decorating a Christmas tree, I love it all. However, Christmas music is definitely my favorite way to celebrate.

That is why I was ecstatic when I found out that Legacy, Heritage High's vocal jazz ensemble, was going to be singing holiday tunes at the White House. As a Christmas fanatic and a new member of Legacy, I was speechless. Plus, on top of everything else, we were going to the place from which our country is run!

I was beyond excited, and everyone else was too. Now, when we asked if we would be able to meet the Obamas, we were told that we would not be able to. Yes, we were disappointed, but we decided to count our blessings and cherish the opportunity.

Of course, my living situation was considered, and so that things would run smoothly the morning of the big day, my mother and Mrs. Stewart agreed on my sleeping at Mrs. Stewart's house the night before and the night of the trip. No matter what, this blessing was not getting taken away!

Once the day arrived, I, Mrs. Stewart, and my fellow ensemble members woke up before the cock crowed so we could head to Washington D.C. After leaving her home, stopping for breakfast, and meeting the rest of the ensemble at Heritage High, we were off for the trip and the surprise of a lifetime.

After a few hours of talking, sleeping, and everything in between, we arrived in the nation's capital. We spent the first part of our day seeing some sites, including Madame Tussauds Wax Museum, and eating a very fulfilling meal. Once that wrapped up, we began to make our way to the White House. Of course, with the building being so important, security is top notch.

So, we had to undergo a screening to enter. I will definitely say that anyone who was not a "touchy feely" person put that away during that time, because it was so cold that we were huddled up like a football team during a time out. Thankfully, we were successfully cleared and got to step onto the lovely (and warm) premises.

Since we were early, the ensemble was able to enjoy a tour of the differently themed Christmas trees that were there. After witnessing the gorgeous, meaningful, memory-filled trees, we headed downstairs to freshen up and prepare for our vocal presentation. Once the time came, we climbed the stairs for show time.

As the night went on and we performed song after song, passing individuals stopped and partook in our unfamiliar vocal ability mixed with familiar holiday tunes. The fact that I and my fellow classmates were able to bless others with the gift that God had given us was priceless. I truly consider it a Christmas gift sent straight from heaven. What I did not know was that, that night, the Father had more gifts in store.

Being lovers of music and excellence, we made sure to perform every set as if it were our last. By the time our holiday program had been completed, we had performed three sets that were each over twenty-five minutes long. So, even though we were all happy that we had helped spread cheer through our voices, we were also happy that we'd be putting our sore feet up and sleeping on the bus soon.

However, rather than being able to grab our coats and walk slowly to the bus, we were asked to come into another room. Even though a nap on the bus and comfortable, cushioned seats were calling us, we were obedient and made our way to the room. Once we got there and sat down, we were informed that President and First Lady Obama would be gracing us with their presence—we would get to meet them face-to-face.

That's right! A young woman who was homeless and in poverty would be able to meet the "leader of the free world." When this registered, I did not know what to do or how to react. Trust me, the others were freaking out too. However, the positive commotion turned into awe when we heard a joyful welcome upon seeing the Obamas standing before us.

Now, according to the Oxford Dictionary, *awe* is defined as, "A feeling of reverential respect mixed with fear or wonder." This perfectly describes the emotions that ran through my mind as we got to sing for them and shake their hands. The fact that I, Amber Brianna Kathlene Gardner, from Newport News, VA, was able to meet these individuals who had earned so much honor and respect, blew my mind.

I truly wondered how in the world this could happen for someone little like me. The only answer is divine favor sent from God above. That is why I give no one else the credit for that but my King, because it was truly a gift from Him alone.

Of course, with my Savior being the loving Father that He is, that amazing present was tied with a ribbon of testimony and remembrance when we were informed that we would be taking a picture with them as well. Til' this very day, I have that photo, which was sent to Heritage so we could all have a copy.

As time has gone on, various family members, associates, and classmates have seen the photo. Some family members even made themselves personal copies for their own enjoyment.

It has become a testament to one of the wildest and greatest seasons of my life. A time where someone who felt like nobody began seeing that your worth is not in what you have, but if He has you.

Another dose of favor that opened my eyes to this is when God decided where my post-secondary education would be and how it would come about. Trust me, He definitely made a point with this, because He did it in a way that broke all of our world's "rules."

"MUSTARD SEED" MIRACLE

In the book of Genesis, there is a very well-known couple who were born as Abram and Sarai but left this Earth as Abraham and Sarah (See Genesis 17: 5, 15). God promised Abraham that he would be "the father of many nations" and that this vow would be fulfilled through a son, Isaac, birthed by Abraham's apparently barren wife, Sarah (Genesis 17:19).

Now, even though God had showed himself to Abraham previously, this was still something that seemed to break our world's "rules" since Sarah struggled with pregnancy and their old age. So, when they both heard this promise from God, they laughed (Genesis 17:17a, 18:12). To them, as great as God was, and as much power as He had, they still did not think it was going to happen.

That basically describes my thoughts when I felt God leading me to apply for Hampton University during their on-site admission at Heritage High in the fall of 2012.

By this time, I had decided to put forth some effort towards a successful future and a stable life. Now, I was not perfect, but I was making progress. The growth in my grade point average was proof, which at that time was a 2.82, a nice jump from the 2.52 that I entered Heritage High with. To some, that may not seem like much of a difference. However, anyone who has been in school will tell you that letting your GPA fall is a big mistake because it is easier to drop it than it is to get it up. That is why I was happy to see my progression, but I knew I was going to have to still jump through some hoops to get the scholarships that I wanted and needed.

Even though I earned a 1210 (Math & Reading) out of 1600 on my SAT and a 30 out of 36 on my ACT, I still had less than a 3.0 GPA. So, I decided to address it in the personal essay that most scholarship applications require. In my opinion, it was best to simply discuss the elephant in the room rather than try to beat around the bush. As it says in John 8:32, "And ye shall know the truth, and the truth shall make you free" (KJV). So, I made the decision to make the truth the main course rather than the appetizer.

Thankfully, this strategy did help bring understanding along with a connection between myself and the college recruiters. However, there was only so much that they could do, and breaking rules was not one of them. As much as they wanted to grant me large scholarships due to my resume, test scores, and story, my GPA was in their way.

From, "We can only offer…" to "Due to…" and even "As a result…" I was given reasons why was unable to receive the packages that I needed to attend school, and it did not just disappoint me. It disappointed the recruiters too. One gentleman who was recruiting even told me to contact him as soon as my GPA hit a 3.0. Then he would make sure I got one of his school's top scholarship offers. To be so close, yet so far away felt tormenting, but it was my doing. So, I had to face it.

That is why I was baffled in disbelief when I felt God pressing me to go and apply for Hampton University at their on-site admission at my school. I had not planned on applying anywhere that day, but I did keep additional copies of my information in case an opportunity presented itself.

Honestly, I did not realize it was God telling me to go, or better yet, I did not want to give Him credit. I would just say "something" told me to go. (Thankfully, my Savior is now getting His just due from me.) So, as I sat there feeling this undeniable tug to take a chance after seeing the valedictorian come in with an admission, I decided to put my best foot forward and go for it. The next few minutes were a blur, and before I knew it, I was downstairs in the office where they were holding the interviews.

I am not going to lie. There was part of me that felt like I was wasting my time. But, I had already put myself out there and there was no time for backtracking, especially once I was told I could come in for my interview.

Now, for those who have not gone through the interview process recently, allow me to refresh your memory about its feel. Imagine being questioned in an interrogation room with your transcript as the evidence. That is the amount of pressure, and then some, that's present. It did not help that I knew my credentials did not meet Hampton University's standards. As a result, I had no idea what would take place. All I knew was that I had nothing to lose.

So, the interview began, and I introduced myself. The interviewer looked at my resume and started asking me different questions about various things she saw. With every question, I did my best to answer them honestly while also giving off an air of self-value. As I responded to every question and request for me to expand upon something, I saw a positive view of me form in her mind. It took on a brightness that went from her soul to her smile.

She began to share with me how she respected the fact that I tackled the mistakes I made. Also, she appreciated that I was upfront about it in my essay and did not try to skim over it. Those things, along with my SAT and ACT scores, left a very positive impression on her. With all of that, I still did not feel that I would overcome that obstacle, especially when I was the one who built it in the first place. However, as Proverbs 3:5 says, "Trust in the LORD with all thine heart; and lean not unto thine own understanding."

As a believer, I have had to learn that we must not only trust in God regarding our trials. We must also have faith in Him when it comes to our blessings, even when they do not come how you planned. I will pause, though, because I am getting a little ahead of myself.

So, we are back at the interview, and the recruiter is loving the drive and presence that I have shown her. I can tell that I have made an outstanding impression and shown a magnificent light. But that GPA still has not changed. No matter how anyone looks at it, Hampton University letting in a student with a 2.82 GPA is considered risky. Not only is it a risk, but it is one that many would feel is not worth taking. That is why, 'til this very day, I know that what happened next was nothing but God.

It is still almost like a dream. We were sitting there having this great, honest conversation. Then the time came for her to make her final decision. Now, as I already said, technically, there should have been little to no chance for me to become a student at Hampton University. So, I was very surprised when I saw her eyes shuffling repeatedly back-and-forth, left and right, seeming as if she was having hard time deciding what to do.

As she did this, a silence fell over the room that previously was not there. It was as if she was making a choice that would change the course of history. Ironically enough, when I look back on it, there was a course of history being changed: mine.

It was changed by one statement: "You know what? I'm going to let you in."

Now, when discussing *surprise*, Boris Pasternak stated, "Surprise is the greatest gift which life can grant us." With the moment that I just described being completely unexpected, it was a surprise that I will never forget. However, that was only the beginning. Even further shock and wonder would be coming in roughly four to five months, and it would all start at a revival.

KINGDOM CONNECTIONS

So, I don't know about you, but I was always taught to be careful regarding how I treat others. Like it says in 1 Peter 4:9, "Be hospitable to one another without complaint" (AMP). Also, due to what I was taught and my own life experiences, I learned to "keep it real" or be honest. Thankfully, in late January to early February, I was able to see the outstanding effects that those practices can have.

It was about a month into winter and I was trying to wrap my mind around the idea of college. Since many schools that I applied to were not able to provide me the amount of financial aid I needed, I decided to audition for Norfolk State University's choir so I could get a scholarship.

To me, it was a safe plan that would get me a bachelor's degree on a budget. However, as Isaiah says, God's ways are not our ways. In other words, we have different plans than He does, and His began to unfold on the way back from a revival on a Friday night.

Now, at my home church, it was the custom to have an individual take on the role as the host or hostess while the guest was ministering. As a result, the guest preacher, Pastor Larry H. Davidson, was being escorted by Windell to his hotel. It just so happened that out of the goodness of his heart, Windell was dropping us off as well. This was where God put his plan into action.

So, we were all in the car and started talking about how we were hungry. Since Windell had to pass by a Sonic to take us home, we decided to get something from the drive-thru. As we were ordering our food, we began discussing Davidson's background. He shared how he was a Hampton alum and founded "His Chosen Sounds," the Hampton University gospel choir. This truly caught my attention because: A) I love to sing, and B) I had just gotten an official acceptance email from Hampton University.

You see, even though I apparently had been accepted to Hampton during the on-site admission interview, there had been some complications. Due to my information being lost, I had to reapply and wait an additional three to four months to know if I was 100% accepted or not. However, as they say, "It's not what you know, but who you know."

So, as the conversation went on I saw how kind, generous, and kingdom-minded this man was. He did not only claim to be a follower of Christ, but he lived it as well. Now, I know some people who have experienced offenses behind the four walls may doubt what I am saying, but trust me. What happens next proves it.

The weekend continued to go well with Davidson teaching a Saturday seminar for Day 2 of the revival. It truly kept showing itself as an uplifting experience, and that is because it had an uplifting guest. Sunday acted as even further confirmation of this. He brought forth an amazing sermon, and the entire ministry was able to be blessed plus edified through his lively, strong words and spirit. We were able to lift God up and accept the true Word being given. Then, things shifted from lively and strong, to strong and specific. Davidson began to mention my name, sharing his thoughts of me, and he introduced me to another Hampton alum in front of the entire congregation.

Words cannot describe what I felt at that moment. As someone who has had to battle insecurity and feeling unwanted, and still has to put it in its place sometimes, the fact that someone spoke so well of me in front of everyone was a breath of fresh air. It completely knocked me off of my feet.

As me and the other alum met in the aisle, tears began to fall from my eyes. It was a gift from God that I held and still hold close to my heart. Little did I know, this gift was about to be joined by many others in ways that I never saw coming.

WON'T HE DO IT?

According to History.com, Valentine's Day was founded in the 5th century and named after an historical Christian. Of course, over the years, it has taken on various ideas, practices, and signs from romance, to giving flowers and chocolates, to even hearts and roses.

For some, it is their favorite holiday. For others, it is just another day. Then there are those like myself, who are somewhere in the middle. This is why I never thought I would receive such an amazing act of love, from love Himself, on Valentine's Day weekend.

It was near Valentine's Day weekend in 2013, and I was living life as usual. Since I was determined to go to college in spite of my finances, I had an audition lined up for Norfolk State University's choir, because scholarships were given to members of the traveling choir. I was grateful because at the end of the day I would be able to get my degree regardless of my income. Plus, I would have a chance to start over and begin anew.

That is why I truly did not know what to expect when I received a letter from Hampton University. Of course, I knew that I had been admitted because they'd sent me the email notifying me. However, I was not expecting anything else from them since my admission email came after their scholarship consideration deadline. As a result, I had no clue what it said or was regarding, but you cannot expect to make it to the end of the road if you do not take steps in faith.

So, I nonchalantly opened the letter and began to read. Word-for-word and sentence-to-sentence, I read further and further down the piece of paper. With every word my eyes got bigger and with every promise a larger smile formed on my face. What was technically impossible was becoming possible. What I thought could not happen was taking place. What I thought was foolish was revealing itself as favor. Hampton University was offering me their Presidential Scholarship.

As long as I maintained a 3.3 GPA, my tuition, room, and board would be covered. That, along with the state financial aid and two smaller scholarships I was receiving, allowed me, a student with less than a 3.0 GPA and no home, to attend a private university for free.

Now, I don't know how anyone else would have responded, but I was as happy as a child getting a surprise party on her birthday. I immediately went and told my mother, who was also ecstatic and who started worshipping God in joy. She had every right to give Him the worship too, because He deserved the credit and the glory.

I was like Moses when I applied to Hampton University. Not only did I have dirt in my past, but I did not trust that God would look past my restrictions. For Moses, it was stuttering. For me, it was having a lower GPA than many competitive institutions wanted. Regardless, God looked past my shortcomings the same way he looked past Moses'. He showed me favor despite my baggage and mistakes.

As with any testimony, it is best to share it at the right time. However, with all my excitement and glee, I could only keep it between me and a few others for so long. So, that Monday, I told the school administrators who I was close with and a few others who had shown their support. Before the end of the school day, over half of the school knew about it. It was like breaking news. Almost no one was uninformed of the blessing.

Funny enough, even though I am someone who loves people and attention, I didn't quite know what to do with all of that. See, I much prefer being the center of attention when I have worked for it and/or saw it coming. This hit me like a whirlwind.

It's kind of like when a celebrity is all over the tabloids because of personal family business. Some may say that they should be happy because it is free publicity. However, the actual person may feel a little different because privacy is priceless. Regardless, it continued to spread, and it caused many interesting, fun, and, at times, hilarious encounters. One that comes to mind occurred with Mrs. Stewart.

WHEN IT RAINS, IT POURS

It was the day before the auditions at Norfolk State and I was ready to go. To me, it was best that I still go out for the choir so I could have a good back-up place in case the scholarship with Hampton fell through. Mrs. Stewart, however, saw things a bit differently.

I remember sitting in the music room in front of her computer. She was doing a carpool for students who were auditioning. I turned around and asked her where we would all meet up the next day. She paused and gave me the most puzzled look. Then she said, "Didn't Hampton offer you a Presidential Scholarship?" I told her, "Yes." Immediately, she answered me like a parent telling their child they can't have a cellphone and said, "Then, you ain't going."

Let me tell you; I tried to argue my case like a teenager trying to get a car. See, safety has always been one of my top priorities. No matter how good things look, I prefer having a back-up plan in case things don't work out. However, she was not trying to hear it. She is a woman of wisdom and faith, and that faith was in full effect.

Another interesting interaction was when Chowan University visited Heritage High for their own on-site admissions. It was not long after I received my scholarship from Hampton University, and it was still a fresh topic among the student body and faculty. As a result, it came up during a discussion I was having with a Chowan representative, who didn't believe me since I had less than a 3.0 grade point average. So, I went and got my scholarship letter as proof.

Even though I don't feel that it's good to worry about other people's opinions, I do have to fight the urge to prove others wrong. Thankfully, I have seen progress in that area, especially with opinions changing every day. What is most important is that you follow the true purpose and path that is divinely set for you. However, I was concerned with hushing their mouths and any doubt they or I had at that moment.

So, I grabbed the letter out of my locker and walked back to the library. There, I handed it to the representative to read for himself. In my mind, it felt like handing a relative my report card to prove that I had earned all A's that semester. It was nerve-wrecking!

As I saw him look up-and-down the sheet, hundreds of looks went across his face, from confusion, to understanding, to finally, surprise. Then he slightly nodded his head, letting me know that he was done reading. After that, he looked up and said, "Well, if they want you, we do too."

Less than six months earlier I was worried about how I would be able to pay for college. In roughly a couple of weeks, I went from worrying to having two universities offering to cover almost all of my college expenses. So, you could imagine that I was baffled.

In the end, after going back and forth for a little bit, I decided to choose Hampton University. It was definitely against my plan to stay so close to home, but God is truly one who will make a straight pitch into a curve ball. Who knows what is best and can decipher what will lead you to get a home run? Plus, He's the coach, referee, and creator of this game we call life. Who better to tell us what to do to win?

What I didn't know was that moving up in rank has its benefits, boundaries, and responsibilities. I wasn't going to be fighting with homelessness on the same level, but another struggle that had been unconquered for years would be battled, and the enemy's leader was the person who I'd least expect: me.

WITH FAVOR COMES RESPONSIBILITY

It's funny. At the end of Job, it reads, "Then he died, an old man who had lived a long, full life" (See Job 42:17, NLT). However, no one ever seems to ask or wonder what happened after God blessed him with roughly twice as much as he had before. Even the world says, "More money, more problems." I mean, once you have a bit less material stuff to worry about, you can't hide behind it or use it to avoid bigger issues.

Now, let me be clear. The Lord blessed me abundantly in a very short period of time. By the summer of 2013 I was offered over $200,000 in scholarships from various schools, earned numerous awards and honors, was given almost $1,000 at my graduation party, taken on a shopping spree for college items, given a free laptop, and received a rent-free, two-month stay in my own room with a personal bathroom and walk-in closet.

In my opinion, I was living large, but once I got to Hampton University, there was less space for personal demons to hide. Insecurities can't be ignored so easily when you're put in situations that cause you to look at yourself. One that definitely stands out is when I acknowledged my issue with pride.

See, to me, going to college was a new beginning. I didn't want any previous situations, struggles, or war scars from the battle of life to follow me. So, that meant no one could know my story and that when it came to financial stability and homelessness, it was still being written.

It's ironic when you think about. My testimony is the tool God used to get me into Hampton, but because I was so worried about appearances, I wanted people to think my wallet, not His will, got me there. Sometimes we get like Joseph did when he spoke to his brothers, and we forget that the vision wouldn't have and won't take place without the visionary. Unfortunately, at that time, my pride didn't care.

I went around for four to five months doing my best to make money stretch, using my refund check to make ends meet. I treated myself to some things, but I tried my best to remember that I didn't have the luxury of running to my parents when my money got tight.

I'm not going to lie and say that it didn't bug me sometimes, either. There were times where I looked at people and wondered, "Why do they have that when they don't even appreciate it?" But I had to remind myself that "complimentary" doesn't always mean complete. As Mark 8:36 says, "For what shall it profit a man, if he shall gain the whole world, and lose his soul?"

With that in mind, I pressed through with my head held high and my mouth shut, until a day came in December when I couldn't afford an expense for one of Hampton University's choirs that I had joined. So, I was forced to unzip these lips and let all the baggage hang out. I still remember it crystal clear.

It had only been dark for about an hour and I was walking to Clarke Hall, hoping to catch Mr. Dunkin, the choir director, in his office. When I tell you, I was more nervous than you could ever imagine. The idea of revealing to someone at Hampton that I didn't have it all together was nerve-wrecking. Having been stung by rejection, isolation, and insecurity so many times, I felt like I needed *extra* protection. What I didn't realize is that that protection can easily morph into pride, because even though many don't admit it, we all need a helping hand sometimes.

However, I was still learning that, which was why I was outside Clarke Hall shaking like someone who was in five-degree weather. Thankfully, I was able to stop worrying and make my way to his office to ask if I could come in. He allowed me in and I sat down across from his desk feeling like a witness in an interrogation room. Then he asked me that fatal question: What did you come to speak to me about?

As I opened my mouth and my heart poured out like the Nile River, I felt a feeling of vulnerability that made my pride drop to its knees. The reality of having to trust someone new and remove the mask that I felt I'd been wearing successfully for four months was frightening, and it caused the wells of burdens I'd been trying to bear to almost overflow.

Apparently, that potential flooding was evident to Mr. Dunkin because, before I could finish, he told me to stop because I was getting emotional. Then, he gave me his response. Now, being the "knowledgeable" person that I am regarding people, I expected sympathy or pity from this man. However, he actually was frustrated because I waited so long to tell him. This was a relief to me because he could have easily said, "So what?" If he had, even though it would have hurt, I technically couldn't have been upset because it isn't part of his job. Thankfully, he loves his job and his students, and that showed on that night.

That is the big difference between doing what you're meant to do versus just working. When it is what you are meant to do,

95

others are helped and encouraged to find their purpose as well. You walk in it. You talk in it. Your actions reflect it and your motives support it. Rather than it being a job, it is a mission. Mr. Dunkin was one who confirmed that.

Well, as a result of these things being present in him, his mission with me deepened. He worked with me so I could participate in the concert and gospel choir. Now, I still had to eventually pay my part like everyone else, because with grace comes responsibility. Both are needed to survive.

This led to my pride being cracked a little bit, but this was years full of pride from seeds of fear and hurt. It was a strong tree whose roots ran deep. More waves and winds of truth would be needed for it to be uprooted. That is where Mrs. Amanda Wright and Monica Parker came in.

KINGDOM KINDNESS

Now, according to some estimates shown on Time.com, 80% of students will change their major at least once before they graduate. This is understandable because for many, college is the time where they discover or begin to walk in who they truly are. I have even known some students who did not choose their major until their junior year because they did not want to waste time studying something they were not going to pursue.

However, with my scholarship only lasting for four years, I chose Journalism as my major as soon as possible. Looking back, I do wish that I had sought God before making that choice, especially since He opened the door to Hampton in the first place. Thankfully, He meant it for my good.

Since I chose my major so early, I was able to knock out a good number of classes needed for my curriculum during freshman year. One of those classes was "Intro to Media Writing", which was taught by Amanda Wright. Now, being a teen from "the 757," a.k.a. Southeastern Virginia, I was not used to being around a bunch of well-connected people, let alone being taught by them. The fact that I had taken a class with Adam Brown, who'd worked with various celebrities and networks, was shocking enough, and Wright picked up right where Brown left off and continued to blow my mind.

Not only had she worked with Inside Edition and been featured on different networks, but she also covered various mind-blowing situations, from radical storms, to murder confessions, to even 9/11. She glowed with beauty, spoke well, possessed intelligence, held her head up high as a black woman, and believed in God! I felt like I was being taught by a living, breathing example of what I wanted to be one day.

This was probably one of the reasons why I was so frustrated when my money got tight and I did not have enough money to purchase one of the class's requirements. Even though I received refund checks, they only went so far, because they were the only source of income I had. Once I purchased a laptop to replace the one I was given, one-half of the money was gone. So, I had to put my pride aside again and let her know what I was dealing with behind the scenes.

I found myself outside of the classroom door one day explaining my financial situation to her and the effect it was having on different parts of my life, including my education. Her response was so full of poise and kindness. It was like class and love ran through her blood stream. I quickly recognized during our conversation that the ability to sense one's gifts also ran through her blood stream.

The fact that she had known me for less than a year and asked me if I had ever thought about writing a book shook me. She had no clue that two other people had asked me that same question in my lifetime, and honestly, I don't think she would have cared because she was speaking the truth in her heart, while also confirming my purpose from the God we serve.

This led me to begin my initial manuscript for this book. Now, I'll keep it real. This book and that book are complete opposites, but I truly believe her question put everything into gear, and she did not stop there. Not only did she lift weight off of my pockets and unknowingly push my dream of writing a book into motion, but less than six months later, she also helped me find a place to lay my head.

See, even though I had received so many blessings so quickly, there were still things that my mother and I had to overcome, and homelessness was one of the top things on the list. Since I was still concerned about what others said, I still had not shared my situation with many people. This resulted in still carrying a strong secret as well as a sad stronghold. However, secrets can only last so long, and once again I came to a point where I felt backed into a corner. So, I had to ask for help once again.

This required my pride getting benched and humility becoming my star player. That included running my plays by others and also letting them join my team. I had to simply put down my reservations and do whatever was right to win this championship called life. Due to wisdom, I try to not run valuable plays by those who can't handle it, and I prefer to not have just anyone on my team. That is why those who truly meet that criteria will always be my MVPs.

One who I'll never forget regularly used her coaching abilities in my life. Her character was trustworthy, and so was her opinion. Plus, I knew she had my best interest at heart. No matter what, she kept it real and always offered a helping hand. She was a walking, breathing example that the Proverbs 31 woman really existed. Her name was Caroline Douglas.

Like many other people who have strongly impacted my life, I met her at Hampton University. During the hustle-and-bustle of classes, newfound freedom, and the potential freshman fifteen, she allowed me to take off my mask and be vulnerable during my less glamorous days. In other words, she was one of the first at Hampton to see behind the scenes.

It's like with movies and plays. We as the audience love to see the finished product, but few of us ever consider the work it took to get there. Actors and actresses go through hours of research, training, make-up, and sometimes even stunts to give us an authentic, honest result. This is how it was with my life. I did not mind individuals seeing my maturity, knowledge, and ability to save & make due. But I'd rather them think I learned these things out of preference, not necessity. It's one thing to do it because it is cool. It's another to do it out of survival.

Thankfully, God used various people to help my desire to be common transform through the realization that I was chosen, and when you look in the Word, those who are chosen should not stand in pride or fear. They should stand in humility and favor. I simply had to learn to accept it, and people like Davis were who God used to make it happen.

One major time that she was used was in the spring of 2014. It was almost the end of my freshman year at Hampton University, and everybody was getting their summer plans together. For some, the plans involved interning. For others, it included a job. For a few, it even included a vacation. However, everyone's life and plans do not play out the same way, which is why some may not be surprised that I did not fall into any of those categories. Due to not having money, I had no idea what I was going to do or where I was going to stay during the summer.

That's right. It had been almost a year since I started attending Hampton University, and my mother and I were still battling homelessness. As much as I loved HU and appreciated the fact that it had provided me with an escape, the summer returning reminded me of my harsh reality.

So, I began weighing my options to try to figure out where I would call home for my summer "vacation." Now, I did not want to go to "everyone and their momma" asking for help because of my pride and my past. I knew that even though Hampton had opened new doors for me, the history of my past actions may try to follow me.

This led to looking at various avenues and finally deciding to simply choose the road that would give me a place to stay and help my education. So, I went ahead and took out a couple of small student loans and registered for two summer session classes at Hampton University. That way, I was able to earn some credits and live in a place where I felt comfortable.

Now, I'm not going to act like I had no reservations regarding this. I was a bit concerned about doing this because it would result in me having student loan debt in future. Due to this concern, I decided to get advice from someone who could confirm if it was a good decision or not, and Caroline Douglas was on that list.

I went to her office one day and spoke to her to see what she thought about it. I was thoroughly relieved when she gave me a "thumbs up" and said she felt it was a good decision. Anyone who has had to make an important decision knows that it feels great to get confirmation. It lets you know that you're not tripping.

With that being taken care of, I now had to only find somewhere to stay for the few weeks in between the last day of the spring semester and the first day of the summer session. That's where Wright came in once again with her wings spread and a solution in hand.

Now, I am going to be very honest. I had always seen her in an academic setting. So, it never truly crossed my mind that she possibly held other positions off of campus. However, like all of us, she wore different hats and had numerous layers. This allowed her to have a good number of connections, which is how she was able to aid me in my situation.

You see, her husband had recently founded a ministry and was its acting pastor. This alone shocked me, and the shock increased when she told me that her friend and church member, Monica Parker, knew about my situation, and had decided along with her family to let me stay in their home during those few weeks.

To this day, this blessing still blows my mind because it further showed me that love is not extinct. Sometimes it may feel like it's endangered, and that it why the Lord's love must be spread through testimony and lifestyle. Our actions are part of the solution, because people are quicker to believe in a Father who has loving children.

It is because of this love through Douglas, Wright, Parker, and my grandmother that that problem was completely solved. Thanks to my grandma's kindness, I even had somewhere to stay for the month between the end of the summer session and the end of the fall semester. With them opening up their homes to me, I was able to press through one of my first summers on my own in peace.

Not only did God provide, but He further healed me and my grandmother's relationship as well. I was so grateful and joyful that I couldn't shake it and didn't want to. What I did not know was that another healing was about to start soon, and even though it would not be comfortable, it definitely was necessary.

STEPPING INTO SUBMISSION

As time went on, I began going through an extremely repetitive cycle: I would have a problem, either divinely sent by God or of my own doing, complain repeatedly and pout, and He would make a way. Whether it was a professor giving me an extension, money being provided, or a word of encouragement, the blessings kept coming. Sadly, since I felt like I had no closure with God, my version of gratitude was not very strong and did not last long.

It was like I was a wife who would not work on her marriage due to a grudge she had against her husband because of one of his previous decisions. However, the Lord knew what to send to provide counseling that would help my perspective to shift and our relationship to heal.

The tool that was sent was a program headed up by Rashad Campbell Jr. and his wife, Catherine Campbell. We met as a result of my singing on a praise team run by my friend, Greg Collins.

You see, Campbell is a campus dorm director and a strong believer. Being that he not only wanted to strengthen his relationship with God, but also wanted others to get to know Him, he held monthly worship services in his dorm. This is where I received my first taste of the essence of their spirits, honesty, and minds, and this flowed right into the program which helped me start towards freedom.

Sadly, even after getting a nice peek at what God was bringing into my life through my education, counsel, and relationships, I was not satisfied. I still viewed the cup as half empty, instead of half full. This continued without much change or interruption until almost the beginning of my junior year. The months before then were truly powerful because they led to me stripping off my defenses with people on Earth and with my Father in heaven.

See, during my time away, I had begun to recognize how much those who were home meant to me. I also began to draw closer to Mr. Campbell through various conversations over the phone. From laughs, to "real talk," and everything else in between, he lent an ear and offered words of sound advice. This led to a trust that was truly of God.

As a result, the calls grew from words of advice to biblical lessons from God himself. I began calling whenever I needed that uplifting. It was amazing, but I can imagine it was a lot. I mean, anyone who knows me or has met me before will tell you that I can hold a conversation from here to kingdom come.

With all of that and with the Campbell's working with others, I can imagine that it felt like a lot at times. That is why I was not very surprised when he asked me if I wanted to officially join his program and be taken on by Susan Grant.

Now, I had already known Susan for about 1.5 years. We initially met at a fellowship for a Christian organization that she co-founded in 2014 and is now heading regularly. Thankfully, during that initial introduction, she showed me an essence of strength, kindness, and humility, things that I felt I had lost. As that year and a half passed, I had various encounters with her and her mother, "Aunt Sharon." Each single one showed me that she was true to herself, others, and the God that she served. To make it plain, she practiced what she preached.

That is why my response when asked if I wanted to join the program and allow Sarah to disciple or spiritually mentor me was simply, "Yes."

So, in December 2015, Susan I signed a covenant which basically stated that I would regularly take off my mask and be honest with Susan about what was going on in my natural and spiritual life. That meant no struggle, complication, fear, or situation was off limits.

She would offer advice, counseling, and 100% honesty to help me figure out the problem(s) and overcome the adversity, even if the problem or adversity turned out to be me. Also, at times, I would read books and write essays on their content. Then, we would discuss what I learned from the chapters and how I thought it would aid me in my everyday life.

It basically was guidance and oversight that was put into place to help me move forward until I was able to stand a bit more on my own. I say that because even if you are not in a program, you still need and want some aid at times. A major issue, however, was that at first, I was a bit of a brat regarding my guidance.

See, I did not think that I needed to let Susan know about my decisions about personal things even though I had gone through unhealthy cycles regarding those things for years. However, when it came down to something I should be praying about, I would normally come to her because I trusted people more than God. I basically wanted to be accountable and receive guidance when it was convenient.

As it says in Proverbs 3:5-6, "Trust in the LORD with all your heart; do not depend on your own understanding. Seek his will in all you do, and he will show you which path to take" (NLT). Sadly, my old bitterness and "unanswered" questions about why things had not gone my way made trusting God almost a foreign concept to me. As a result, my relationship with the Father and those who followed Him became pretty tough. It took various conversations, book chapters, Bible verses, and other tools to get me out of this trap, and it was not easy because I was the one holding the key.

However, I had become so comfortable in bondage that the idea of freedom did not seem worth it to me. I felt like there were too many questions, "if's," "and's," and "but's" for me. With my mind being this way, I allowed myself to begin to value my version of stability more than salvation and God's will.

Thankfully, God knows just when to work on a wall and who will be able to help you tear it down. The secret is that, normally, the person who helps your walls fall had similar bricks in theirs also.

So, as time moved on and the pride, as well as the stubbornness, began to come down, growth began to take place. Now, I am not about to lie. It didn't happen overnight. There were plenty of dragged out discussions, unnecessary responses, instances of denying the truth, and other rebellious actions. I am not proud of it, but I am thankful that I have moved forth.

Even today, I am not perfect. There are times when I have to double-check my responses to make sure I am being respectful and considerate. Also, I have to remind myself that accountability is not someone trying to control you. It is someone caring for you.

In the end, it comes down to what is most important to you. If the answer is your desires, good for you. I only hope you are ready for the consequences that come with them. On the other hand, if it is your destiny, get someone to help you prepare for the battles and the blessings, and please remember that it is all worth it.

That is what I had to do, and it has helped me grow into the woman who is writing to you today. The woman who's walking in her God given path and who is trying to help others follow His steps as well.

EPILOGUE (BIGGER THAN ME)

Life at this time is still unfolding. I graduated from Hampton University in May 2017 with a Bachelor of Arts in Journalism. Also, I was able to remain on the Dean's List for my entire undergraduate career, graduating with a 3.26 GPA.

Along with a great education came great savings, because I owe less than $6,000 in student loans as a result of my scholarships and financial aid. This allows me to have much less to think on. God also provided a great place to think on it when He had my mother and I move into our own apartment in early 2015. Yes! He delivered us from homelessness once again, and I am eternally grateful.

My relationships with my parents and natural family have healed. It is not a fairy tale all of the time, but it is not a nightmare either. We simply take it day by day.

Also, issues that I had with previous believers have healed as well. Trust me, it took time, but it was worth it.

Looking back, I would not change a thing, because my testimony can help someone else. I know it is not in vain. That fact alone puts a smile on my face. Now, I have my "up" days and my "down" days. Moments when I smile and times when I frown. When those days come, I have to just press through and command my soul to trust the Lord. It definitely flexes my faith muscles, but experience is where one's strength comes from.

When my mom was in the hospital, I had to trust Him. When I didn't have my own home, I had to trust Him. When something happened in my body, I had to trust Him. That is how I am able to share my story today. There would be no need to tell you how I got stronger if no weights existed.

In the end, I had and have to remind myself that He is in control and is using me for a marvelous plan. In layman's terms, "It is bigger than me."

ACKNOWLEDGEMENTS

I first want to thank my Lord and Savior, Jesus Christ. If it were not for His indescribable grace, mercy, favor, and love, I would not be here today. Also, I want to thank those who He put in my life to help me make it here. From their uplifting smiles to their awakening truths, I am grateful for it all.

Also, I want to thank my spiritual family, including my kingdom big sister, Sarah Gatewood, and my kingdom parents, Mr. and Mrs. Raymond Cullen. Your honesty and dedication is a priceless gift that will always be in my heart. You saw what God had in store for me before I could see it myself, and your lifestyles and families helped open my eyes to a freedom that I had never seen.

Next, I want to thank my natural family. Even though we've had our ups and downs, we love one another and that will never change. Our valleys simply help us grow stronger and we must take that strength with us wherever we go.

I also want to thank my teachers and professors. Arcelia Simmons, you were a rock in my life when I felt like the storms of life were washing everything away. You allowed God to use you in such a way that it still blows my mind, and I will be forever grateful. Thankfully, that support and love was also shown to me at Hampton University through professors such as Allie Butler, Brett Pulley, Omar Dickerson, Carol Davis, April

Woodard, and many more. When I did not want to admit that I needed a shoulder to lean on, they pulled me in and let me know that theirs was always available.

Not only was I able to receive love and support from those over me, but I gained it from my peers as well. There's Lakita Wiggins and Kison Osbourne, who I've known since middle school. They helped me maintain a social life, not allowing me to let my struggles be my main focus. Then there is Alexis, my little "cuz", whose family has been there for me and my mother through thick and thin. Also, there's Neidra, who has helped me grow and supported me to the point that it still blows my mind. Next, you have Andre and Ellarese, who encouraged me and helped me have a kingdom cut-up or two so I wouldn't confuse being a believer with being boring. There are so many names, I cannot even list them all. It truly shows that God can use whomever He wants, regardless of their age.

I also have to thank Hermelinda Miller of Project Discovery and Sis. Sheila Green. These two women have encouraged and helped me in various ways, from conversation and open ears to constructive criticism and action. The fact that they have stuck by me through everything I have been through is a true blessing from God himself.

There are many more who have had an amazing impact on my life, and I want to say thank you to you all. Without you, I don't know where I would be. Please know that I am forever and eternally grateful, and every correct step in my purpose is my way of saying, "Thank you."

Made in the USA
Middletown, DE
22 June 2025

77336510R00070